An Unsung Hero
Coming of Age in the Dust Bowl

William M. Forsythe

Red River Press of Texas
Dallas, Texas

To my heroes, Jimmy and Velta

To the great grandsons, Alexander and Liam, and the great granddaughters of Jimmy Ray—Emma, Grace, Lilley, Macy, Layne, Anna Reese, Mariela, and Elizabeth—I dedicate this story of an unheralded man who provided for his family and gave them a future that was better than his own without expectations of thanks, reward, or responsibility . . . he did it because he loved them.

All rights reserved. No portion of this book may be used without the sole permission of the copyright holder except by a reviewer who may quote brief passages in a review.

The information contained herein is the result of numerous personal private conversations between the principal, Jimmy Ray Lewis, and the author over the last decade of Mr. Lewis' life. Where possible, additional information was collected through interviews of other family members and friends, correspondence of Mr. Lewis, and publicly available historical material. Some of the names have been changed out of respect for the privacy of the individuals mentioned in this book.

Copyright © 2014 Michael R Lewis
All rights reserved.

FOREWORD

The following pages reflect the memories of Jimmy Ray Lewis more than three-quarters of a century past. The passage of time and the accompanying wisdom of age have not dulled those childhood and early teen experiences during one of the most tumultuous times in US history. Despite being born in the heart of the Dust Bowl and experiencing the hardship of the Depression while suffering a community's rejection due to tuberculosis, Jimmy recalls the joys and simplicity of his life in the Texas Panhandle. Readers will enjoy the recall of a time and values long past, but the real story of his life is family, community, selflessness, and integrity—characteristics which forged a man, an era, and generations to come.

At a time of manufactured demand, constant stimulation, and instantaneous gratification, Jimmy's description of the early 20th century life and technology may seem naive. Iceboxes, phosphates, poultices, and mumbley pegs are the lexicons of by-gone days. In our effort to cram as much experience as possible in every waking moment, we have forgotten the true pleasures of walking barefoot, a homemade apple pie, or a shave at the local barbershop. Reading these pages is a humbling experience given the advancements over the last three-quarters of a century. Few would trade their childhood for a year spent in a sanatorium, but many of us yearn for a simpler life not filled with deadlines, rush hour traffic, and mindless television.

Jimmy Ray Lewis was my grandfather—affectionately known as Papa. He was an Unsung Hero—a Railroad Man— a vocation steeped in history and romanticism. To a young boy growing up in Dallas, Papa was my hero. Just as Papa had spent his boyhood summers with his uncles, my parents packed my bags and dropped me off to spend a week or two each summer at his house in Wichita Falls. While the town and the importance of the railroad have changed over the years, I eagerly anticipated my visits and the trips to the train yard where I sat on PaPa's lap in the huge engine of a diesel locomotive. Being a fly on the wall, listening as colorful old men spun their tales of life on the railroad was priceless.

That is not to say that Papa did not value a day of hard work. He believed that pride in one's self and true independence required effort, trial and error, failure, and accomplishment. Every summer my duties included mowing the lawn, cleaning the pool, repairing and building trellises for his patio, and helping him in his carpentry shop. While a loving grandfather, he was not an easy taskmaster. His core values, forged in his early life, passed first to his son and then to me, have shaped me as a man as well.

Jimmy Ray Lewis' early life was not easy, but it was a simple and happy time for the young boy. His account of growing up in Texas, despite the hardships of the time, has been tempered by the wisdom of a septuagenarian without the cynicism of lifetime grudges or hurts. His story is not only a family treasure, but also a gift to generations to come.

Michael R Lewis Jr
May 30, 2014

Table of Contents

1 TEXAS ROOTS   1

2 SETTING THE SCENE   11

3 LIFE IN CHILDRESS   24

4 ELEMENTARY SCHOOL YEARS   41

5 PLAY TIME   48

6 GHOSTS, WITCHES & CIRCUSES   56

7 RUBBER GUNS AND NIGHT GAMES   64

8 THE WEEKENDS   69

9 COUNTRY COUSINS   84

10 ROOSEVELT IS ELECTED   102

11 THE WINDS COME   110

12 JUNIOR HIGH SCHOOL   117

13 THE SANATORIUM   125

14 HOMECOMING   132

15 WORLD WAR II BEGINS   136

16 WICHITA FALLS   142

ABOUT THE AUTHOR   148

William M. Forsythe

1 Texas Roots

Life at the turn of the 20th Century, especially in the area of the Panhandle border between Texas and Oklahoma, was rugged. Francisco Vasquez de Coronado described the Panhandle as "a great sea, without a stone, a bit of rising round, not a tree, not a shrub, not anything to go by or find your way." The land to the naked eye appears flat, but a closer examination reveals an expanse of llano broken by gullies, arroyos, and mesas. The pastures of short prairie grasses invaded by patches of wind-blown hardscrabble were better suited to ranching than farming, especially around the Red River where rainfall was spotty throughout the year and non-existent in the summers. From time to time in the spring and early summer, savage thunderstorms unloaded buckets of water on the thirsty soil too quickly to be absorbed in the ground. The spontaneous, but temporary rivers carved still more gashes in the harsh land as they ran south to the Gulf of Mexico. In the winters, zephyrs of frigid winds swept across the plains, gaining momentum as they traveled down from Canada. Channeled by the Rocky Mountains to the Panhandle, the stinging blasts pummeled any inhabitant foolish enough to brave the open prairie.

At the turn of the 20th Century there were no paved roads or automobiles; people still traveled by horseback and wagons. Farmers and ranchers occupied most of the land and cowboys regularly wore pistols to kill the ever-present rattlesnakes. The few small towns scattered throughout the region struggled to exist and often disappeared during a hard winter. The Ft Worth & Denver Railroad, one of the primary stimulants for the settlement and farming of the Panhandle, was the only reliable transportation over long distances, although few traveled far. Most people in those days lived and died within one hundred miles of their birth.

Napoleon Bonaparte supposedly said, "There is no such thing as accident; it is fate unnamed." I have always believed my destiny was decided long before my birth. My father, Virgil Lee Lewis, returned from the killing fields of Europe in 1918 to begin a life-long infatuation with the Ft Worth & Denver Railroad, initially as a locomotive fireman, then as an engineer.

It was a fickle association, at times one-sided when the company would furlough Dad for months without explanation, regret, or even a promise of future relations. Nevertheless, Dad was smitten with the big iron machines that dominated the lives of the Texas Panhandle inhabitants. At the turn of the 20th century, the railroad provided seeds, land, and access to faraway markets to farmers, well-paying jobs to working men, and dreams of exciting possibilities to every school boy who watched in wonder as the mighty engines thundered past.

Before I could walk, Dad carried me on his shoulders as I looked in wonder at the size of the powerful steam engines that dominated the rails in the 1920s and 1930s. He roared with laughter when the engineer, knowing we were nearby, released clouds of steam and smoke to billow from beneath the wheels accompanied by the loud shrieks of the train whistle and his little boy. Dad loved everything about the railroad and I am my father's son.

When he did not have work as a fireman or as an engineer for the Ft Worth & Denver, Dad was a gambler and an occasional bootlegger when he did not have work as a fireman or as an engineer for the Ft Worth & Denver. In his thirties, he was a big, barrel-chested man with thick shoulders and arms, the result of shoveling coal for hours on end to feed the tenders of steam engines as they hauled freight and people across the Panhandle of Texas. He never welched on a bet, turned his back on a friend, or walked away from a fight.

My father was a fastidious man, despite his work in a physically grueling, often dirty, and always-greasy environment of a steam engine cab. He bathed every day when he finished work. He insisted his white shirts be starched and ironed and his three-piece suit brushed before appearing in public. He was a little eccentric—replacing pipe tobacco in his ever-present briar pipe with a half cigar. The burning end of the cigar extended two to three inches above the bole to the level of his eyebrows causing the smoke and ashes to waft over his forehead like wind over an airplane wing.

Originally from the hills of Scotland, via the green fields of Ireland, our ancestors on both sides of the family have been Americans since the late 1700s. My great-grandfather, William Franklin Lewis, formerly from Alabama, and Mary Jane King, his Mississippi-born wife, moved to Hill County, Texas shortly after the Civil War ended. His son, George Peter Lewis, born soon after in 1869, married Nettie Long who was from another family that moved to Texas from Nebraska seeking a new start. The ever-restless George, called "Popeye" by those who knew him, moved to Chickasaw Nation in Indian Territory where my father, Virgil Lee Lewis, was born October 22, 1896. My father's mother died when he was fourteen and his father never remarried.

Dad at five foot, eleven inches was a tall man for his generation and carried one hundred-eighty pounds, mostly through his upper body. His chiseled features, black hair, and strong, straight nose, combined with a devil-may-care attitude, made him popular with both men and women. Like most men of his generation, Dad had little formal schooling. He worked as a cowboy, farmhand, and laborer until volunteering in 1917 to fight against the Germans in the first Great War. After returning home and knowing he was not suited to farming, he found work as a fireman on the Ft Worth & Denver Railroad, working out of Clarendon, Texas in 1920.

Mother's family experienced a similar migration. The first ancestor to America from her side of the family was James Forsythe from Londonberry, Ireland sometime before 1750. James married Margaret Vale, the daughter of English emigrants. Over the next several generations, the family moved first to Virginia, then to South Carolina, Tennessee, and finally by the late 1800s, to Texas. My Grandfather, Joseph Forsyth—the "e" having been dropped from the family name two generations earlier—was an educated man who taught at the Decatur Bible College around 1900 before buying a farm near Snyder, Texas. Also an ambitious man, Grandpa Forsyth traded his Snyder farm for a larger place near Texola, Oklahoma in the part of the country called the High Plains. He then bought a second farm near his first property and a third farm just across the border in New Mexico. My mother, Mary Fay Forsyth, was born on February 6, 1900, in Vernon, Texas near Turkey, Texas, the hometown of her mother, Sarah Alta Card. When Mom met my dad in 1921, she was living with her family on her dad's farm at Texola.

I do not know the details about when Dad and Mother had first started courting, but I suspect that he had heard of the shapely young, single daughter of another farmer from his father, Popeye. Nature being what it is, they fell in love and married in Texola in February 1922. I suppose it was somewhat of a miracle because two people could not have been more dissimilar in personality. Dad was excitable, rambunctious, always ready for a good time, but could be arrogant and edgy on his bad days, while Mother was responsible, steady, and somewhat of a prude due to her religious upbringing. The Forsyths were always active churchgoers—faithful members of the fundamentalist Church of Christ denomination for generations. Dad usually accompanied us to church, but I was never sure that his heart was into it.

Dad was working with his father to raise maize and cotton on Popeye's Texola farm when my parents married. He had been laid off by the railroad—the first of many furloughs that happened over the next two decades. I was born April 15, 1924, just a few months before Mother's father, Joseph Forsyth, died. One of my Mother's older brothers, John, moved to the farm in New Mexico while a second brother, Coke, took over one of the Texola farms, and the family sold the third farm. Mother's other two brothers, Homer and Ernest, bought and worked another farm in Texola, so the family stayed physically close. After Grandpa's death, Grandma Forsyth moved to Turkey, Texas to stay with her family for a couple of years before returning to Texola and moving in with Uncle Ernest.

When Grandpa Forsyth got sick, he kept asking for Mother. Travel by horse and buggy was so slow that she did not arrive before he died. No one knew what he wanted to tell her, but she suspected it was the location of his buried money. In the early 1920s, most people did not trust banks, so they buried their money in fruit jars and chests for safekeeping. No one knew if he had hidden money; however, Grandpa had owned the three farms outright so the family surmised that he had saved a considerable sum. If so, he died without telling anyone the location of his savings and his suspected treasure was never found.

Shortly afterward, the railroad recalled Dad to work in Amarillo, so Mom, Dad, and I moved there. Popeye, in bad health, sold his farm and moved with us. Grandpa Lewis died in Amarillo the following year (1926) from "locked bowels," what today might be called severe constipation. In those days, doctors were not trained to do that type of surgery and there was no other cure for his condition.

At the time when Grandpa died, the bodies of deceased people generally laid in state in the house where they had lived until it was time to bury them. One of my relatives carried me into the living room to see the body of my Grandfather before the funeral, but I was young and do not remember much about it.

After a death and the body lying in the house for days, it is not surprising many people moved from their home to another dwelling, saying they could never lose the memory of seeing the corpse there. My family feared neither spirits nor dead people, possibly because they were farmers and used to the death of animals or because they had faith in God and the hereafter. As a consequence, I did not learn about ghosts until years later.

When the railroad transferred Dad six months after Popeye's death, we moved from Amarillo to Childress. Traveling was slow in the 1920s because most of the highways were scraped-dirt lanes glutted with deep ruts and bottomless potholes. When night caught us in mid-trip and Dad could not see the road ahead, we spent the night along the road. I slept in the car and Mother and Dad spread quilts on the ground beside the car to sleep. When we got to Childress, we moved into a duplex. A redheaded girl about my age lived on the other side of the house and we played together most days.

I remember, as a young boy living in Childress that first time, wrapping a ball of string around my left hand. When Mother noticed what I had done, my hand had turned blue from the loss of circulation. She quickly unwound the string. I thought I had ruined my hand! For the first time, I also noticed my fingers were different lengths.

Many people had nicknames in those days more so than today. I do not remember why, but the neighbors called me "Wild Onions" when I was little. My uncles and the family called me "Doodle Bug" and later just "Doodle." Dad's friends on the railroad called me "Little Lardy" because Dad's nickname was "Lardy."

Having what he thought was a steady job, Dad bought a 1925 Buick. We kept the car in a neighbor's garage across the street since they had no car and we had no garage. The car had a top, but was open on the sides and back. Curtains, made with a clear material in the center so you could still see outside the car, snapped into rivets at the top and bottom of the window. The windshield wipers were manual. The temperature gauge—a thermometer—was in the radiator cap. During the winter, Dad drained the radiator every night to keep the engine block from freezing, only to refill it the next morning before starting the motor. Almost everyone who owned a car did the same thing, although few people had cars.

The Ft Worth & Denver Railroad fired Dad in1927. It happened when the switch engine he was working on ran into the depot, knocking the building flat. Why the railroad bosses fired Dad, the fireman, instead of the engineer who was in charge of the engine is anyone's guess, but employees did not question management in those days. One official thought the firing was unfair and hired Daddy the following week to work in Silverton, Texas to watch engines for the railroad.

As an engine watcher, Dad's job was to ensure the steam engines always had a fire with plenty of water in the boilers so that they were ready to go the next morning. If an engine cooled, the metal would shrink, and water from the boiler would leak into the motor's cylinders, locking the brakes so that the train would only creep down the track. Dad's job required him to stay up all night, constantly checking the water in the boiler and the temperatures of the steam of each engine. If either the temperature or the water were low, he would add coal to the fire and/or water to the boiler.

Since Dad's work was seventy miles away, we moved from Childress to Silverton to be closer to Dad's work. We rented a small house with a big backyard where I had my fifth birthday.

Our milk and butter came from a cow Dad bought. One morning, I tied an old dishpan to our cow's tail and let her out of the backyard. I thought it was funny to watch Mom and Dad, running down the road, yelling at the top of their lungs, chasing that old cow with the dishpan banging and clanking behind her. At least it was funny until she was caught and brought home. That was the first time Dad spanked me. Mother had handled that job very well up until then.

In the summer of 1929, Ft Worth & Denver called Dad back to Amarillo and reinstated him to his old job as a fireman. When he arrived at the depot wearing a green felt hat, he was told that the railroad would rehire him, but only if he got rid of the hat, which he did. He celebrated the turn of good luck by seeing his first talking movie, "The Birth of a Nation." With his old job back, we moved once again—back to Amarillo from Silverton.

While we lived in Amarillo, I got my first dog, a collie. He was a beautiful animal and went everywhere with me. Lacking imagination, I named her "Collie." We lived across the street from a school and I would go over there to swing. Collie would start me swinging by jumping up and pushing on my back with her front legs. I hated to leave her behind when the railroad transferred Dad back to Childress later that year, but we had no room for a dog and Dad found a good home for her with a neighbor.

After the move, Dad traded our Buick for an almost new 1929 Graham Paige. The people on the east corner from us were the only other family on our block with a car—an Essex. In the next block west of us, two families owned cars—one a Whippet and the other an Oakland. The Oakland was the first car that I had ever seen with a speedometer that went to 100 MPH. Our Graham Paige, while not as fast, had four forward gears, including one called "Grandma Low" for use when you really needed to pull in low gear. Since there were few paved roads in those days, that low gear was necessary to avoid being constantly stuck in the mud.

The Graham-Paige was a fancy car. Behind the front seat was a pullout to hold a sack of tobacco. The armrest on one side in the back had a leather book to hold cigarette rolling papers and the armrest on the other side had a leather book with a mirror in it.

Uncle Homer also bought a new Pontiac auto that year. He and his family came through Amarillo from Texola on their way to California to see Mother's sister, Aunt Lurie. There were four adults and two kids squashed into the car for the trip—Uncle Homer, Aunt Edna, my cousins Lura Fay and Addie Ruth, Uncle Ernest, and Grandma Forsyth. Driving all the way from Oklahoma to California and back was quite a trip in 1929—about 2500 miles, taking at least four days each way if you stopped each night and did not have any problems on the road.

Later that year, Uncle Homer was in a horrible accident. In addition to working with Uncle Ernest on the farm they had purchased together, he was the manager of the cotton gin in Texola. A cotton gin separates the picked cotton from its outer cover—the "boll"—and seeds. The gin is a big machine that is open on one end where the picked cotton is loaded. The cotton then moves through several turning cylinders of sharp hooks or knives to separate the bolls and seeds from the cotton fiber. One day at work, the gin clogged due to a piece of scrap caught between the turning cylinders. Without thinking, Uncle Homer reached in to remove the obstacle. The gin knives, still slowly turning, caught his right arm and pulled him headfirst into the machine. By the time one of the workers pulled him loose, the sharp blades had sliced his arm to the bone and continued spiraling, slashing all the way up to his shoulder and across his back.

We rushed to Erick, Oklahoma, which was the nearest hospital to the gin, to find Uncle Homer in critical condition and not expected to survive. The doctor sewed up his arm, but left the cuts exposed to the air to heal. Not bandaging those cuts may have saved his life. He never got an infection, but his arm was stiff for years. He could not milk with that hand for a long time.

As luck would have it, while we were in the hospital visiting Uncle Homer, the hospital admitted someone with diphtheria. As a result, the doctor vaccinated me and the other kids at the hospital. At that time, patients with diphtheria, scarlet fever, or typhoid fever were immediately isolated from the public and quarantined. When the government officials quarantined a house, no one could come or go from the house for at least thirty days—a major imposition if you worked a regular job. Consequently, most people avoided reporting any illness that might lead to the family's quarantine.

While we were in Erick seeing Uncle Homer, Dad received a call from Oklahoma City about Aunt Gad, his baby sister, who had also been in an accident. We immediately drove from Erick to Oklahoma City on Highway 66. Because the road was not paved much of the way, we were often stuck in the mud. Dad, cursing loudly with Mother's approval under the circumstances, almost burned out the clutch of the Graham-Paige getting in and out of mud holes. It was a bad time for the family, but everybody lived. Except for that incident, I was not around Dad's sisters as I grew up, so I do not know much about them.

2 Setting the Scene

Following our move back to Childress in 1929, Dad told Mother that we were there to stay. By that time, my little sister Alta Jean had joined our little family and moving three times in one year had taken its toll on the family.

Many people have forgotten that the present-day Childress, originally named "Henry," competed with another town called "Childress City" to be the county seat in 1887. Residents of the county voted for Childress City, but the railroad threatened not to stop its trains in the new county seat. The compromise was to move the county seat to Henry as the railroad wanted and change its name to "Childress." To calm feelings, the railroad gave all of the residents of Childress City free land in Childress and helped move all of the buildings to the new community. Childress City disappeared. The newspapers did not report how the former residents of Henry felt about their new name.

The previous house in which we had lived in 1925 had burned down, when we returned to Childress. We moved initially into a duplex next door to the burned house for six months, then into a small house located just a block from the railroad tracks and two blocks west of the depot. The railroad track ran east and west, splitting the town down the middle. All the streets running east and west were Alphabetical avenues—Avenue A, Avenue B, and so on. Main Street was perpendicular to the railroad track and split the town north and south. The streets running north and south were numbered streets—First, Second, Third, etc.

The intersection of the railroad and Main Street divided the town into four quadrants naturally named Northwest, Northeast, Southeast, and Southwest. Northwest was generally considered to be the more affluent, i.e., the "best" part of town, followed by Southeast, Northeast, with Southwest considered to be the poorest neighborhood. We lived in the Northwest section, along with other railroad employees, because the entrance to the railroad shops opened on Ave C NW.

The railroad was the reason that Childress, population of about 6,000 people, existed as a town. The rails, originally built through the old OX Ranch, opened up the Panhandle of Texas for small farmers and ranchers. The town, being halfway between Wichita Falls and Amarillo, was also a natural location for a major railroad terminal. The railroad was the town's largest employer with its employees being among the best-paid residents. Most of the other people in the county farmed or ranched.

The railroad furloughed Dad in 1930, the cutback due to the Depression finally hitting home in Childress. Before 1929, things had been booming and Wall Street was the place to invest. Some people even borrowed money on their homes to invest in stocks. When the economy collapsed and the stock market dropped, loans went unpaid and people lost their homes. Companies fired thousands of workers and there were no jobs for anyone. If people had money in one of the banks or finance companies that failed, they lost their savings too.

When furloughs and terminations first started, they began in the Northeast region of the United States and primarily affected those who worked for large industrial companies. As the Depression deepened, however, unemployment and wage cutbacks spread across the entire country, wreaking hardship upon everyone. No matter where they lived, people lost their jobs. For instance, on our block in Childress, only three families on either side of the street had someone with a regular job. I am sure the rest of the country was the same or worse.

Most of the people we knew lived in rented houses and did not suffer the loss of a home with the loss of their jobs, but they did lose their income. Men who were able to keep their jobs had their pay cut as companies lost sales and profits. The government seemed powerless to do anything to fix the trouble; the politicians spent their time arguing about the role of government in the crisis. Some Congressmen wanted to create programs to help; others were afraid any assistance would lead to socialism. While the Washington politicians argued and debated during the early 30s, more families suffered, growing desperate for any solution to return to normalcy.

There were so many Ft Worth & Denver employees laid off—some with a lot more seniority than Dad—that he and Mother worried he might never be called back to work. Fortunately, the company decided to build a track named the "Denver Northern Railroad" which would run from Childress to Pampa. Texas's quirky laws in those days allowed many little rail lines, even though the same financial tycoons owned most of them. Nevertheless, the construction of the Denver Northern turned out to be a blessing for us.

Although the Ft Worth & Denver had always been union, management decided to build and run the new line with non-union employees. Had the new line followed union rules, Dad would have been hired as a fireman or not at all since he lacked seniority. Instead, he was lucky enough to be hired as an engineer, which was more important and a higher paying job. The work lasted about a year, allowed us to catch up on some of our bills, and provided Dad with a year's experience as an engineer. When the Denver Northern job played out, Dad looked for other work as our savings were depleted.

Driving a car was a luxury we could no longer afford. Since we did not have the money to even license the car in 1930, Dad stored it in the garage by putting bricks under the axles to raise the wheels off the ground. He told me that the rubber tires would rot if the car were just parked in the garage with the tires sitting on the ground. He also drained the water from the radiator and the motor oil from the engine. In the thirties, there were no thermostats and the only available anti-freeze was alcohol-based. If a car got hot, the coolant just boiled away. When the coolant was gone, the water would freeze if the temperature was below 32°F and possibly crack the engine block. Not wanting to take a chance on ruining the motor, Dad drained all of the fluids. He poured the used oil on the street to keep down the dust.

We were not the only ones who had cars on bricks; they were all over town. Walking, which had always been common, became more so since those who owned cars put them in storage as we did. From 1931 to 1935, Dad stored our car in the garage for various periods and we walked wherever we needed to go. The only families who drove cars had fathers who had not lost their jobs and received a regular monthly salary. Only a few families in Childress were in that position.

At times over the next five years, we were unable to pay the electric bill or rent. Our rent was $8.00 a month and electricity was about $3.50 monthly. In order to be able to stay in the house when money was tight, Dad had the electricity turned off and negotiated with the landlord to pay the rent when times were better in the future. During the

An Unsung Hero: Coming of Age in the Dust Bowl

Depression, having the electricity disconnected when there was no money for the bill was common. When that happened, everyone used coal oil or kerosene lamps for light. The lamps were not as bright as electric bulbs and they fumed and smoked as they burned, but they were better than being in the dark. My family was lucky, since we only relied on oil lamps occasionally and never for months at a time.

Times are tough when people cannot afford to use city water. All during the Depression, our neighbor who lived two houses down carried water from our outside water faucet to their house for cooking, washing, and drinking. Neither the husband nor the wife could find steady work and depended upon friends, other family members, and occasional odd jobs for what money they had. The neighbor between us was afraid to give our unemployed neighbor water from his house since his family took in washing and ironing for their living; if they failed to pay their water bill, they would lose their only source of income.

Men who did not know where to go or where to turn for work began riding freight trains to distant towns looking for work. Most often they rode in the boxcars, but occasionally hung onto the ladders on each end of the boxcars or lay on the rails that extended beneath the boxcars. Men, young and old, rode the trains across the country, getting off in the towns where they hoped to find a meal or a little work.

The train-traveling men—"hobos"—gathered in semi-permanent, sparse camps called "Hobo Jungles" or "Hoover Towns" near the railroad yards at night. We had one outside Childress for more than a decade where fifty to seventy-five men at a time sat around little campfires, cooked beans or coffee in empty tin cans, and sometimes shared a rabbit or a chicken from someone's back yard.

Boys too young to shave and old men with grey scraggly beards, their balding heads covered with dirty fedoras, bowlers, or caps—all of them waiting for the next train going in either direction to a new town and the possibility of a job could be found in the Hobo Jungles. No one stayed long in Childress. As soon as they found out there was no work, they caught the next train out.

Since we lived by the tracks, one or two strangers came to the back door every couple of days and asked if we had any chores that they might do for a meal. We never had any work, but Mother always found something to make a sandwich for them. Sometimes it was just potted meat or bacon and eggs, but she could not bear to not give them something. I heard that hobos would leave signs or marks that they used to identify those houses where the residents would treat them kindly, but I never saw anything around our house out of the ordinary. Maybe they just took their chances and hoped Mother was a Christian woman with a kind heart.

There were stories of railroad police who abused those riding the rails. I do not know if the stories were true, but I never saw anyone at Childress hit or beat a hobo. Most railroad men understood the plight of the men, knowing that "there, 'cept for the Grace of God go I." Consequently, the trainmen, including most of the train guards, generally let the riders alone unless they were drunk, looked like they might steal something, or otherwise made trouble. Of course, if push came to shove, a railroad man would put someone off the train even if he did not like having to do so. In such desperate times, no one would risk a job and his family's livelihood for a stranger.

Hobos were not the only people who had a hard time in those days. Some families in Childress were wholly dependent upon credit given to them by local merchants. The few national chain stores wanted cash only, but the locally owned stores did not have much choice but to sell on credit and hope they would get their money eventually; their products would rot on the shelf otherwise. Merchants were in the same boat as their customers—dependent upon credit from the wholesaler to buy supplies. Everyone worried about a chain reaction where one failure would domino throughout the whole town. "What can I do?" "How will I feed my family?" These questions were on the minds of men and women, fathers and mothers, and especially widows who had children at home. The economy in the Panhandle was destined to get even worse before it got better.

In some parts of the country, the government sponsored sewing rooms and canning plants for widows and women whose husbands could not find work. The pay was $30 monthly. The general rule for government employment was only one job per family. The clothes and food produced from the sewing rooms and canning plants was donated to those who could not find work. We did not have any canning plants or sewing rooms in Childress, probably because the town was too small.

By the end of 1931, Dad had found a job working for a road contractor building the highway from Childress to Pampa, Texas. The contractor had previously built artificial lakes—probably what you would call "big ponds" or reservoirs today—to supply water for the construction. Large gasoline pumps and temporary pipes supplied water as the work progressed from one town to the other. The pumps were critical because if they broke down, the work stopped. Dad kept the pumps going, working alone at night to ensure that they were ready for the next morning.

My Dad took me along many nights. I had a ball out in the country at night. While Dad worked, I threw rocks at jackrabbits or skipped flat stones across the water of the pond. Most nights, before I went to sleep in the backseat of the car, Dad told stories to me of growing up in Indian Territory or about his time at war. When it was chilly, he sat with his arm around me, smoked his pipe, and spun tale after tale of cowboys, soldiers, and old railroad men.

The pumping job played out after a few months and Dad began hunting for another job. We stopped our electricity, but were able to pay the rent of our bills for a while with the money he had saved from tending the pumps. Dad and I never again spent as much time together as we did during those evenings; I hope Dad enjoyed them as much as I did.

The grocery bill for the four of us—Dad, Mother, my sister Jean, and me—ran about $15 a month, even though Mother planted a garden and canned vegetables and fruit. After Dad had been out of work for a while, he decided to try picking cotton, even though it had been years since he had last worked in a cotton field.

The desperation of those times is difficult to imagine. I remember seeing fifteen to twenty people—men, women, and children with bonnets, straw hats, and bandanas on their heads, dressed in every fashion—chopping weeds in the cotton fields on the outskirts of town. They were people who, before the economic downturn, had good jobs—clerks, business people, farmers, and railroaders. Sometimes, whole families worked in the fields, anything to make a dollar and get by another day.

In the fall, the same people filled the same fields, hoping to pick the mature cotton. Cotton grows in a "boll"—a hard protective hull around the cottonseeds and the white cotton fiber. Picking cotton meant pulling the whole boll and the number of pounds of bolls picked determined the amount of pay received. Pulling bolls paid less per pound than picking cotton from the boll, due to the weight of the seeds and hull in the cotton boll, but it was faster.

Pulling bolls required finding a field that needed pickers. The fields closest to town always filled up first. In addition, everyone in a family might work. The greater number of pickers reduced the time needed to harvest the field and the pay of each picker due to the shorter time. The greater number of pickers also meant a shorter season of employment.

After finding a field that needed pickers, the real work started. The farmer gave each picker a cotton or burlap sack about ten feet long with a strap sewn to the open end which looped over the head and one shoulder. The sack stretched out, filling with bolls, as the picker moved down the row, dragging the sack behind. When the bag was full and weighed, the farmer would deduct the cost of the sack from the total pay for the day.

Most pickers wore gloves to prevent the sharp edges and points of the prickly leaves from cutting and puncturing their hands as they pulled the bole from the dried plant. Some people stooped over to pick, others crawled on their knees, all the while dragging a sack that got heavier as they went along. A picker would go down one row and up another until the sack was full. When the sack was full, the picker carried it to the weighing station, usually at the farthest corner of the field, for weighing. After weighing, the picker got a new sack and started over on an unpicked row. People picked from morning until dusk. They brought their own water and food if they wanted to drink or eat.

When the picking season started, the cotton gins would open and provide a few jobs, along with jobs at the compresses, but the employment was seasonal. At that time there were no machines to do the job of picking cotton—those came much later. The prices of cotton and wheat fell so low during the Depression that it was hard for farmers to get ahead, even with bumper crops. Caught between the forces of supply and demand, the farmers plowed more acreage to produce larger crops that, in turn, produced more supply and another drop in price.

Farmers generally borrowed from the banks or stores before and during the growing season. When the crop finally came in, they repaid all of their debts at the bank and general store in order to have credit available for the next year. A single bad crop could wipe away years of struggle and hard-earned savings, making it hard to pay off their farms or put anything away for the future.

At the end of his first day in the field, Dad came home stooped and bent—his muscles so tight he was unable to stand straight and so sore he could hardly move. It was a bad day; Dad had not pulled enough bolls to recover the cost of his cotton sack. He told Mother, "That's it. I'll never pick cotton again. I can make more money playing poker and dominos in a night than in a week of picking cotton."

Mother, being a Christian woman, was not happy with his decision, but knew he was right. It was one of those times when married people agree to disagree and to keep their opinions to themselves.

An Unsung Hero: Coming of Age in the Dust Bowl

Dad was an excellent domino and poker player and had a fabulous memory. He could riffle through a deck of cards, hand the deck to a bystander, and then call out each card in its proper sequence. It was not just cards that he was good at remembering, either. He could repeat a long list of numbers almost as well. Once while working on the railroad, another engineer bet $10 that Dad could not walk from the caboose to the engine and, from memory, write down every initial and number on the freight cars in their proper order. Dad won the bet. With his memory, Dad could remember every domino or card as it played and who had turned it. His memory gave him a real advantage over the other gamblers who thought he was just lucky.

Dad was disappointed that I did not have his faculty with cards. When I was six or seven, he taught me to play poker and dominos, expecting that I would love the games as he did. He was a tough teacher and a worse winner. Once I learned the rules, he treated me like any other player and teased and ridiculed me when I made the wrong play or forgot the cards or dominos already played. I became a decent player, maybe better than most, but I never enjoyed the games like Dad. Most importantly, I did not like risking my hard earned money on a poker hand!

Being away from home with nothing to do and having bigger incomes than most, many railroad workers became big gamblers. There was always a game at the local YMCA where the men stayed on their layovers. The Y had a cafe with a separate room where they played poker every day.

We lived in a great location for Dad to begin his occupation as a gambler since the Y was only about a block and a half from our house. Most of the Amarillo and Wichita Falls engine men either stayed at the YMCA or the boarding house across the street from the Y; only a few stayed in the caboose since it was cold in the winters and hot in the summers.

We were able to get by on Dad's winnings for a while, but it was a tough way to live. Although he sometimes played for thirty-six hours straight, he did not always win. I could tell by the way he walked home if he had a good day at the table. He walked really fast to get more money when he was losing; but he was in no hurry when he won—just strolled along happy as a lark, anticipating Mother's reaction when he put his winnings in her hand.

The poker games in Childress were private, invitation-only affairs and tolerated by the sheriff because, first of all, the players were predominately railroad men and the railroad was important to the town and, secondly, the money involved was small even by 1930s standards. Since the fellows knew each other, no one wanted to "hurt" a player, letting him lose so much that it might affect his family. Most pots were under $10 and a big winner might take home $20-$30 after playing all night. There were no markers or IOUs allowed—if a player did not have cash to meet a raise, he either dropped out or borrowed from a friend sitting at the table.

Dad's advantages were that he was very good at remembering cards, he never drank, and he played with the same group of men for years. Strangers were not welcome— players either worked on the Ft Worth & Denver or were friends of a regular in the game. When Dad and I talked about poker playing when I was older, he explained that, most of the time, he played the other players, not the cards. He determined by the way they played whether they had the cards or were trying to run a bluff. For example, Goofy, one of Dad's friends, would act totally opposite to what he had in his hand.

An Unsung Hero: Coming of Age in the Dust Bowl

If his cards were good, he would make small bets and never raise until the last few hands; if his hand was a likely loser, he always bet aggressively to get other players to drop out. In the ten years Dad played with him, he never changed his pattern. By watching the same players over time, Dad could tell those who never bet unless they had the goods and the ones who tended to bluff with poor hands.

Dad treated poker playing like the business that, to him, it was. His winnings sometimes were the only way we could pay the rent or buy groceries. Mother kept all of his winnings, doling them out each time he went to play. If he lost and needed more, Dad had to convince Mother before she let him have another stake.

All of the neighbors and the church members knew what Dad did during those days, but they never treated us any differently as a consequence. People knew times were hard, so men did what they could to make money. At that time, gambling and bootlegging did not have the stigma they have today—there was no Al Capone or Mafia supplying bars and speak-easies. The bootleggers in Childress were our neighbors out of a job. When they found work, they quit selling or making liquor until they ran out of work and money.

One time when Mother, Jean, and I came home late after visiting my uncles in Texola, we walked in and found Dad and some others playing poker at the kitchen table. Wow, was Mother mad! She did not say anything when we came in the back door, but sent Jean and me immediately to bed. Dad knew she was unhappy when she stomped through the house, ignoring the other men—an act totally opposite her normal graciousness. The game ended quickly after we got home. I do not know what she said later, but Dad never played poker in our house again.

3 Life in Childress

Even though the economy was in turmoil and my parents agonized over their ability to provide for the family, they kept their worries to themselves. I think their decision allowed Jean and me to have as normal a childhood as possible in those circumstances. I never felt deprived of anything or that my family was any different from other families. I suspect that is true for most generations. The father of my best friend, Bobby, worked in the Freight department of the railroad, so Bobby had as much (or as little) as I did and that was true for our other friends. It was also a time when you shared what you had if the others did not have as much.

In the early part of the decade, men who kept their jobs in the railroad repair shops were cut to three days a week and later to eight days a month. The men who ran the trains—the engineer, fireman, conductor, and brakemen—took cuts in pay when routes were discontinued. However, even after the cuts, railroad operating men still made from two hundred to three hundred dollars a month—the best jobs by far since a family could live on forty dollars.

The best and worst thing about those days and living in a small town was that everyone knew everyone else and felt their hardship when they had troubles. Although government had no programs to help the unemployed or the widows in Childress, the community helped those most in need.

The railroad men were always at the front of the line to give assistance, generally acting before asked. Innumerable

An Unsung Hero: Coming of Age in the Dust Bowl

families found bags of groceries on their porches donated anonymously by railroad men. Trainmen paid for countless critical medical operations. Our neighbor across the street, Alec, was an engineer who never refused anyone in need. I sometimes wonder how much money he loaned to people, knowing the money might never be repaid.

For almost a decade, my dad worked sporadically for the Ft Worth & Denver, furloughed almost as much as he worked. Nevertheless, we were a railroad family and considered one by all of the other railroaders working in Childress, Amarillo, and Wichita Falls. Mother and Dad's friends were like us—sometimes working for the line, other times on furlough. Most of my friends' fathers worked for the railroad and their families were proud of their work.

During the next five or six years, I paid for Bobby's tickets to the movies or the carnival when he had no money, just as he paid for me when I was in the same condition. I never resented it and neither did he. We had good examples in our parents; when someone needed help—whether it was repairing a house or needing groceries for a week—everyone pitched in. A small town was a great place for a young boy to grow up with plenty to do and little danger, as long as you used common sense—a quality in abundance in most kids in those days.

Our house, just a block from the railroad depot and three blocks to the railroad yards, shared the block with eight other houses and, luckily for me, a vacant lot located next to our house. A similar number of houses stood across the street. The houses were small, wood-framed bungalows, around 1000 square feet, with faded paint, low-pitched saddle roofs and small stoops that extended across the front of the house. Each side of the house had at least two double-hung windows—a necessity to facilitate a cooling breeze through the house in summers. Black wire mesh screens that kept out the bugs covered each window and the front and back doors. They were kept open most of the time to welcome any wayward waft of breeze. Home evaporative coolers—called "swamp coolers"—didn't become common until the 1940s when people could afford the electricity.

The lots on which the houses sat were big because land was cheap. Even though the houses sat apart from their neighbors on both sides by at least twenty feet, murmurs and bits of conversations floated from one house to another, making family secrets hard to keep. When one of the kids got a whipping, everyone in the neighborhood could hear the yelling.

Some houses had detached garages in the back (ours did not) and some had fenced backyards (we did); the fences were not fancy or formidable—usually four to five feet high red pickets strung together with wire. Building a fence was simple. It was just a matter of digging a few postholes, setting wooden posts with two-by-fours running at the top and bottom of the posts, and unrolling and nailing a bundle of picket fence from the hardware store.

Gates were homemade of two-by-fours and more pickets and closed with a simple eyehook and latch. The only reason to have a fence was to keep domestic animals in or neighborhood dogs and cats away from a chicken coop. Kids in the neighborhood usually ignored fences and property lines, always taking the shortest distance between two points even if it meant climbing over a few fences and going through someone's backyard.

A narrow dirt alley with deep ruts ran between our house and the house behind us. The garbage truck was the primary

An Unsung Hero: Coming of Age in the Dust Bowl

user of the alley, collecting our trash once a week. Kids also checked out the trash for anything unusual or useful in one of their activities. The streets and alleys around town were mostly dust and packed dirt that became saturated and viscous in our rare rains. A couple of streets downtown had been paved with brick in the 1920s, but paving was expensive and considered unnecessary for the few cars that operated regularly in the town.

Like the grasslands from which they were wrested, lawns by early summer were usually grey, scattered clumps of dead or dying weeds fighting a losing battle with goat-heads—a ground-hugging plant with masses of stickers, each having two or three sharp spines sturdy enough to puncture bicycle tires and the feet of a careless, bare-footed walker.

Our small wooden porch with two concrete steps was big enough for two kitchen chairs set side-by-side. A narrow, pockmarked concrete walk connected the porch to the sidewalk that extended around the block. In the evenings, Dad in his sleeveless undershirt, old fedora, and smoking his pipe, sat on one of our kitchen chairs with its back legs set inside two empty Folgers coffee cans. These allowed him to lean back against the house without the chair slipping beneath him. Mother sat in the other chair or on the top step of the porch, snapping the ends of green beans or hulling peas grown in her garden into a big ceramic mixing bowl in her lap. Neighbors, sometimes with the whole family, who walked by on the sidewalk or the unpaved street, occasionally stopped to talk with another family sitting on a porch. Children played up and down the block—running through the front yards, between the houses, and down the sidewalks.

We lived in a "modern"—meaning we had running water and an inside bathroom—three-room house with a small kitchen. Whenever we needed hot water for bathing or washing dishes or clothes, Dad or Mother lit the gas heater under the water tank with a long wooden match. After a bath, they were careful to turn off the gas because if the water got too hot, it would turn to steam and blow the water tank through the roof. Lighting the heater required striking a match, then turning the gas valve, and placing the lit match in the burner. Matches did not burn long while the gas flowed quickly from the valve into the room. Sometimes, the free gas in the air would ignite with a loud whoosh and an explosion of flames hot enough to singe the hair on the arms of the person with the match. Consequently, Mother restricted me from lighting the heater until I was ten years old.

Most houses were built with wood before World War II; only the affluent could afford brick houses. While there were outside and inside walls like today's houses, there was no insulation in the space between the inner and outer walls to keep out the heat or cold, just open space. Some people put used newspapers and magazines in the space, I think more to dispose of them than for insulation value, but what does a kid know?

The inner and outer walls were wooden planks nailed to two-by-four framing studs. People hung a picture or a mirror anywhere in their house by driving a nail in a wall and never worried that the nail might loosen. Dad drove ten-penny nails in each room to hang our hats, coats, and Mom's Sears calendar in the kitchen.

People covered the inside walls and ceiling with cheesecloth, then pasted wallpaper to the cheesecloth, usually with homemade flour and water paste. In those days, everybody had to know how to wallpaper since few could afford to pay for someone to do it for them.

An Unsung Hero: Coming of Age in the Dust Bowl

We re-papered our house when I was about eight years old. Using wallpaper rolls they had purchased from the general store for ten cents a roll, Mom and Dad carefully measured the distance between ceiling and floor. Then Mother and I cut new strips from each roll as Dad hung the paper. Each strip was a different length because the house had moved and settled over the years since construction. When I put a marble on the floor, it would skitter in different directions because the floor was so uneven. My job was to spread paste on the inside of the wallpaper while Mom maneuvered the cut strip around on the kitchen table. Mom worked with me while Dad hung and smoothed the previous strip of wallpaper on the wall. Jean was too little to help, so she played outside or went to a neighbor's house until the job was over.

Smoothing was a two-step process. Dad would initially drag a three-foot length of a one-by-four board down the newly hung paper strip, pressing on it as hard as possible to squeeze out any excess paste. If he did not smooth the paper as tightly as possible, the paper would not stick to the wall, and bubbles would appear. After a couple of trips down the wall over the freshly-hung paper with the edge of the one-by-four, Dad rolled our rolling pin—the same kitchen tool Mom used to bake bread and pies—over the wall to remove any small air bubbles under the paper. When he was satisfied that the paper was as tight as possible, Dad wiped the extra paste from the edges and swiped it on the wall where the next roll was to go. During Dad's smoothing, Mother stood on a chair with a string at the ceiling line while I stretched it tight to measure to the floor. Then, using the string measurement, we marked and cut the next strip for hanging.

When he finished smoothing a piece, Mother and I had the next piece ready. Dad took one end and pressed it at the top of the wall while Mother positioned her end near the floor, each carefully matching the seam of the previous hung strip. The more paper strips you hung, the faster and sloppier you became. Every home I visited in those days had dried white paste spots on the wall. Nevertheless, wallpaper with all of the intricate patterns was a lot prettier than bare or painted walls.

Papering the ceiling was more difficult and much slower. Dad positioned a plank on two sawhorses that he stood on to reach the ceiling. Walking up and down the plank, he hung the wallpaper on the ceiling as Mother walked beside him on the floor carrying the loose end of the strip. For smoothing, he only used the short one-by-four, not the rolling pin, because it was too tiring to have his arms over his head for so long. Because of the physical difficulty, ceilings always looked worse than walls, but who cared? By the time the ceiling was finished, there was paste everywhere—in our hair, on our faces, clothes, and the floor—but it washed off easily.

The only room in the house with a light switch on the wall was our kitchen/living room. It also had a single plug in a wall near the floor. The other rooms had one light—a single bulb hanging in the center of the room from the ceiling. You pulled a string hanging from the one bulb to turn a light on or off. Sometimes, finding that string in the dark was difficult. I was not tall enough to reach the cord to turn the lights on and off until I was almost eleven.

Until radios became popular, there was no reason to have more than one plug since there were no electrical appliances. Fathers usually added a plug in a room for an electric lamp if needed, but most people did without electric lamps in the early 1930s.

For heat in the winter, we had a gas heater in the front room and the gas cook stove in the kitchen. Lacking heaters,

An Unsung Hero: Coming of Age in the Dust Bowl

our bedrooms were icy cold in the winters! I went to bed, balled up, and shivered under the covers until body heat warmed a spot; and then tried to stay as still as possible. If I moved, I got cold again.

Some of our neighbors burned coal for heat and built a fire every morning in a cold house. People who did not have gas heaters burned coal or wood in heaters with attached stovepipes that discharged the smoke and carbon dioxide through the roof. Like Dad, they knew how to bank a fire to keep it burning all night. In the morning, instead of building a new one, they just added coal or wood, stirred the embers with a poker, and had heat very quickly.

My friends and I played most often on the vacant lot next door—the house having burned down before we moved to Childress. It was a great lot with a cistern in the backyard and an old outhouse that stood on the alley. Before city sewers, residents, especially in older houses, had used outhouses for toilet purposes just like those in the country. When cities laid sewer lines down the alleys, most people simply sat a toilet over the sewer line and built a small building around it. While answering nature's call still required a trip outdoors, the new arrangements were much better than the smelly outhouses they replaced.

The toilet—a round, cast-iron, commode-like bowl with a wooden seat—perched atop a straight eight-inch pipe that extended from the sewer line to about a foot above the ground. When not in use, the front of the seat rose up about three inches; when in use, the seat was down. When the visitor finished, the seat sprang up, flushing, and alerting everyone in the neighborhood.

Nevertheless, that old toilet was great for the kids—boys and girls—in our neighborhood since we never had to return to our houses to use the bathroom. We were sorry when the city finally demolished the old outhouse after complaints from the neighborhood mothers.

When any of the kids in the neighborhood had fireworks, we threw them in the old cistern to make the boom twice as loud. We put our heads in the hole at the top of it to holler and hear the echoes, too. Best of all, though, were the times we set fire to the trash that regularly accumulated in the cistern. The burning trash—mostly wet paper—excreted clouds of noxious black smoke that covered the neighborhood, burning eyes and prompting our mothers to call the fire department. I bet I was told, "Don't do that again" at least fifty times until I finally got too old to enjoy the uproar. Of course, the younger kids in the neighborhood continued the tradition when my friends and I moved on to better pranks.

Childress had a great park where people from around the county gathered for family reunions. When the swimming pool opened in the summers, a dime paid for an all-day admission. In addition to the pool, the park had a football stadium, a track for foot races, a lake, and a play area with slides, swings, and picnic tables.

The willow trees planted around the grounds were fun to climb and the limbs were perfect for making bows. A small willow limb about three feet long was ideal for a bow—easily made by tying a piece of cord on one end, pulling the string as tight as you could to bow the limb, and tying the cord on the other end when the shape was just right. We made arrows from orange crate slats, sharpened on one end with a notch on the other for the bowstring. We did not know how to attach feathers on the arrows, so they were not very accurate. It was the thought that counted.

An Unsung Hero: Coming of Age in the Dust Bowl

Our house was about a mile and a half from the park. Sometimes, when we could afford to drive the car, Mother would take a carload of neighborhood kids to the park. When sliced bread became popular, bakers wrapped the cut loaves in waxed paper to keep the loaf together. The discarded waxed bread papers were perfect for the slide. After three or four people went down sitting on the wrappers, greasing up the metal chute, the next rider had to be ready for a fast ride, quickly getting their feet down at the bottom of the slide to run about ten feet or tumbling on their you-know-what.

The park had monkey bars, a large sand box, and rings to hang from and swing. There was also a push merry-go-round with steel handles. Three or four of us would grab a handle and push as fast as possible to get the wheel spinning, then jump on and ride until it stopped.

When I was older, my friends and I walked to the park every day in the summers. While Childress had a population of less than six thousand people, there were always kids at the park ready to play. Even though we were only eight- or nine-years-old, we were able to care for ourselves pretty well. Our parents did not worry about us playing outside; trouble is hard to find without something to make trouble. In addition, each boy carried a rabbit's foot for good luck. When one of us found a horseshoe, which we did quite often, we took turns spitting on it and throwing it over our left shoulder for more good luck.

Necessity is the mother of invention, so we created our own games. For example, when we found a tin can, we took turns kicking it all the way home; if an empty can wasn't available, we used small rocks although they were hard on your toes if you were bare-footed. Sometimes, we found an old baseball and played catch, usually ending in "burn-out" where each of us threw the ball as hard as possible hoping the catcher couldn't hold on to it.

Some kids played marbles, but I did not care much for that game. Drawing a circle in the dirt was all we needed to play. At the game's start, everyone would put in three or four marbles from the stash everyone always carried in their pockets. Everyone had a "shooter" marble called a "taw" that was either heavier or larger than regular marbles and used to knock other marbles out of the ring; a shooter kept whatever marbles he knocked out. There were always older kids playing who could shoot a marble more accurately and with more power than I could, so I always left with fewer marbles than when I started.

We sometimes played "tracks," a game that required each person to follow in the footprints of the person immediately ahead of them. Sometimes, we would race one another by running a block and walking a block until someone cried, "Uncle." I do not remember ever being bored or unable to think of something to do. Sometimes walking home from the park alone, I would pass a house where kids were playing in the front yard and stop to banter with them. In a town as small as Childress, I quickly met most of the kids my age, especially after school started since there were only two or three elementary schools.

There was a grocery store on the corner just west of our house. Most people in town kept a garden for vegetables and some owned chickens and/or a milk cow; grocery stores mostly handled meat and vegetables that would not grow in Childress. For me, the grocery store was great because of the candy kept in bulk amounts in big bins or wooden barrels in front of the counter.

An Unsung Hero: Coming of Age in the Dust Bowl

Most of the bins had a little wooden keg about the size of a shot glass that measured out candy. When a kid bought candy, the grocer would dip the little keg into the bin and fill it full of candy corn, orange slices, cinnamon-flavored "red hots," candy-covered peanuts, or hard-coated jawbreakers for a penny. Giant suckers and candy sticks of all flavors only cost a penny, too. For a nickel, I could buy a huge piece of chocolate—big enough to share with a couple of my friends.

Store-bought loaves of bread were available for those who could afford a nickel for a loaf. However, most people bought flour in forty-eight pound bags and sugar in twenty-five pound sacks to bake their own bread. Mother made and baked our bread, biscuits, pies, cakes, and other pastries. She cooked nearly everything we ate, creating delicious meals from scratch without the aid of a recipe. Mother had learned to cook helping her mother as a young girl, as did most girls in those days. Most boys learned to fry or boil some things, but never to the skill of the girls.

Everyone canned the fruits and vegetables grown in their garden or they were purchased from a local farmer for eating in the winter and spring months. We never bought jelly since Mother made jams each year, but we did buy sorghum syrup for "hot cakes." Mom sometimes made "mush"—a hot cereal made from white cornmeal—for Jean and me; it tasted like grits that you might eat today. We ground some of the corn from our garden to make cornmeal. Oats for oatmeal were only available from the store, so we did not eat it very much.

Dad did not like any kind of cereal and expected Mother to fix him a full breakfast of eggs, bacon or ham, and biscuits with gravy, washed down with milk from our cow and bitter black coffee every morning.

We only had meat in three or four meals a week because it was expensive. We ate red beans, corn bread, and potatoes cooked in different ways. Round steak was cheapest at twenty cents a pound. When we had meat, it was usually fried chicken from our own coop, ham or pork chops from my uncles' farms, or chicken-fried round steak with mashed potatoes and white gravy.

Milk was five cents a quart and came in glass bottles. Although we lived in town, we had a cow and chickens, along with a vegetable garden, two peach trees, and a blackberry patch. Mother sold some of the milk and butter, but we usually kept the eggs for ourselves. Dad loved eggs—fried, scrambled, boiled, or pickled—and Mother used any extra for her baking.

We did not have a butter churn, so we made butter by shaking a fruit jar until the cream became butter. The process took a good while and a lot of shaking. What butter we did not use, Mother gave to the neighbors. Milk and butter came from local farmers, unless you had a cow, and was not pasteurized. We had one creamery in town that bought and pasteurized milk from local dairies, but few families bought it because it was a few cents higher and tasted different from the raw milk we usually drank.

To make buttermilk and butter, my uncles and other farmers generally used a large crock churn with a dasher going up and down by hand, rather than shaking the cream in a glass jar as we did in town. Until homogenized milk became available in 1943, milk came with the cream having risen to the top of the bottle. Kids were taught to shake a bottle before drinking to mix the cream and milk; unshaken, the top was pure cream. Many a mother raised Cain when someone drank the cream that could be used for whipping cream. It took quite

An Unsung Hero: Coming of Age in the Dust Bowl

awhile to break the habit I developed of shaking a bottle of milk before I poured a glass.

Milk was important to me for more reasons than being a healthy drink. Even though I was only five when we lived in Stanford, it had been my job every morning to lead our cow from our back yard, stake her out where the Johnson grass grew, and bring her home in the afternoon. I also had to keep her water barrel full. In Childress, I had the same chore.

When I was about seven or eight, I earned my first money by collecting empty milk bottles and selling them back to the creamery for a nickel a bottle. I also collected wire coat hangers to sell to the tailor shop, earning a penny for every two hangers.

Dad did not have a regular income until I was eleven or twelve, so there was not extra money for allowances or extra goodies for Jean or me. When we went to the store and could afford it, my folks would sometimes give us a couple of pennies or a nickel to buy candy, but it was not a regular habit. However, I never felt deprived since most of my friends were in the same shape. Like me, they collected bottles or hangers from time to time, but never as regularly as I did, just whenever they needed money to buy something. I kept a piggybank where most of my earnings went and I always looked for ways to make more money.

Prohibition provided another source of income. The United States had passed a prohibition law in 1920 before I was born. Since neither Dad nor Mother drank, I was not aware of the law, particularly since those who did drink never had problems finding liquor. In my early years at Childress, it was still illegal to possess alcoholic spirits in any form or to make or drink spirits except in medicine. Some people, desperate for a drink, began drinking Bay Rum hair tonic,

Vanilla Extract, strained alcohol out of Canned Heat, or paregoric since there were no liquor stores. Paregoric—a tincture of opium—was used to treat diarrhea or sometimes given to babies with colic and a prescription was not needed to buy it.

Other people made home brew (beer) or white lightning (whiskey) and became bootleggers. Even in the midst of the Depression, there were enough people with jobs to keep bootleggers in business. Home brew was bottled and capped, if it did not explode while fermenting. Whiskey was available in fruit jars, small flat bottles without any design or writing on them, or old, used whiskey bottles. The last was my business opportunity.

Bootleggers would pay me a nickel for every empty bottle I found and there were plenty of bootleggers in the neighborhood; I could see four from my house. I never told Mother or Dad about that side of my business. I let them assume the money came from milk bottles or hangars. When I was eight years old, Congress repealed Prohibition, making the sale of liquor legal again. Once the companies started making whiskey, there was no market for used bottles. Some men continued to distill liquor to sell without paying the taxes, but they were not as visible as the bootleggers around town during Prohibition.

There were only a few mechanical refrigerators then and most of them were for commercial use. Few families could afford one for the house. Dad bought our first one in 1937. We kept milk, butter, and other perishable items in an icebox. Our icebox held a fifty-pound block of ice in the top compartment and the food was stored in the lower compartment. As the ice melted, the water ran down a pipe and dripped into a pan; Mother emptied the pan several times each day.

An Unsung Hero: Coming of Age in the Dust Bowl

An iceman delivered ice for the iceboxes six days each week. On delivery days, the iceman and his big dray horse pulled a four-wheeled cart down the street, moved from house to house, and stopped to make deliveries. The ice company provided an ice card to its customers; the card folded in the middle and stood erect like a triangle. On one side, the card had 12½ pounds and 25 pounds; when you turned it inside out, it said 50 pounds and 75 pounds. Homemakers put the side with the pounds of ice they wanted in a front window or on the porch where the iceman could see it from the street.

Wearing a heavy leather apron on his back to keep him dry from the melting ice, the iceman chipped the order from one of the 150-pound blocks in the back of his cart with a big ice pick. When it was the right weight, he picked up the chipped block with a set of heavy steel tongs, slung it to his back, walked into the customer's kitchen, and put the block in the icebox. We got fifty pounds of ice every three days. Whenever the iceman's horse stopped, kids gathered around his cart for a free sliver of ice—moving the piece from one freezing hand to the other as they licked and sucked on the chip.

People in the country did not have iceboxes because they had no deliveryman. To keep their food cool, the farmers' wives put any food that might spoil in a wooden or tin box near a windmill and let water run continuously over the box. If the windmill was too far from the house, they filled window boxes with water and put screen wire around the box to keep flies out. Nothing kept things very cold.

The ice cream man also had a covered wagon like the iceman's rig. The ice cream man's horse, however, wore a fancy leather harness with straps that covered his whole body from neck to tail. The straps had little brass bells that jingled every time the horse moved, signaling the arrival of the ice cream man. The horse stopped every time a kid ran out. A double dipper of ice cream was five cents, so most kids could only buy one ice cream every week or so. In the late 1930s, the wagons and horse teams began to disappear. I never liked the trucks that replaced them as well as the horses.

Downtown had a couple of pharmacies with shelves for sundries and newspapers. Some of the pharmacies had a soda fountain that sold ice cream, cokes, and other drinks like limeade, phosphates, sundaes, and shakes or malts. For fifteen cents, the Soda Jerks would mix up the best banana splits you would ever eat—with dips of chocolate, strawberry, and vanilla ice cream along with whipped cream, nuts, and cherries. I do not remember eating many because that was a lot of money to spend for one thing. During school, the older high school kids gathered at the soda fountains with tables and chairs where they could sit and talk while drinking cokes or eating ice cream.

Grocery stores did not sell ice cream so eating ice cream was a special treat. It took a long time to make ice cream at home in a special hand-cranked freezer, so we only had it for special occasions when the whole family was together. Usually Dad or one of my uncles turned the crank while my cousins or I sat atop the freezer to keep it stable. From time to time, one of the women would ask the men to stop cranking, open up the freezer, and taste the ice cream to see if it was ready.

4 elementary school years

In the 1930s, the State of Texas only required eleven years of schooling to receive a high school diploma. We went five years in elementary school, the sixth and seventh grades in junior high, and years eight, nine, ten, and eleven in high school. With only about 2000-2500 kids in all eleven classes, everyone went to the same school in the neighborhood where they lived. There were not many organized school activities until high school. I started the first grade in September of 1930 after I turned six years old, but I never liked school, as it interfered with my play and moneymaking activities.

My elementary classes had about twenty-five to thirty kids in each room—all of us from the neighborhood. We stayed in the same room with the same teacher for all of our classes. Education then was focused upon reading, writing, arithmetic, and music (singing). As we moved up each grade, we changed rooms and teachers; sometimes we got new classmates from the other classes. Our mothers made our lunches and we had two recesses, one in the morning and the other after lunch. I do not remember ever having homework. When school was over at 2:00 PM, I played with my friends until it was time for chores or to do any paying work I could find. After dinner, I went back to play until it was time for bed.

Education was not a major topic of conversation in our house and my parents never went to my school unless it was for a special occasion like Halloween or Christmas. Because of growing up on a farm and expecting to spend their lives farming, neither Dad nor Mother had gone to high school.

Both could read, write, add, subtract, and do simple multiplication and division, though. In those days, education was intended to be practical, not learning for the sake of knowing. I never saw Dad read anything but the newspaper and Mother read mostly the Bible.

Except for parents, teachers and principals occupied the highest rungs of the discipline ladder. Generally, misdeeds resulted in staying after school, although boys could sometimes elect to take licks—swats on the rear end with a paddle—instead of detention. I always chose detention since it only extended the school day by 30 to 45 minutes. Taking licks hurt, which could lead to tears and further embarrassment. I did not need that.

Most people did not have telephones so, if a child misbehaved, the teachers sent a note about the transgression home with the child for the parents to sign, then the student returned the signed note to the teacher. Mother's handwriting was almost illegible and, by the fourth grade, I could forge her signature. Since neither of my parents went to school or talked with my teachers regularly, I got away with the forgings. That is, until Jean started school and would race home to tattle on me whenever I got into trouble.

Even though I know now we had money problems, my parents never talked about money in front of us or to Jean and me. I eavesdropped on conversations when they visited with other adults when they complained of the hard economic times, especially my uncles and aunts, until they shooed me outside for being too curious. I never thought about being rich or poor or felt that I missed anything because I was no different from my friends whose fathers were also unemployed or only worked when they could. In those days, growing up in Childress was great.

An Unsung Hero: Coming of Age in the Dust Bowl

My friends and I had regular chores at home that we did every day or weekly. In addition to running errands when needed, we usually chopped weeds in the yard and garden and helped around the house. The type of assigned chores depended upon whether you were a boy or a girl. Boys had to learn some things that girls normally did. For example, by the time I reached the fifth grade, Mother had taught me how to properly wash and dry dishes, sort clothes to launder, cook well enough that I would never go hungry, iron shirts and pants, and enough sewing skills so that I could mend a tear or replace a button when necessary.

I had several paying jobs before I was ten. One spring when I was eight, a downtown photography studio paid me to wear a box with my head sticking out of a hole in the top with advertising on the four sides. For two hours on two consecutive Saturday mornings, I walked up one side of Main Street and down the other to advertise the Studio: my pay— three small photographs of me. I proudly took them home to Mother for Mothers Day, the first time I ever gave her a gift paid for with money I had saved or earned with my own work. Mothers Day had already been commercialized by the 1930s as the time for children and husbands to buy flowers and gifts for the mothers in their lives.

When I was growing up, I believe, children behaved better in public then because it was expected. In those days, adults presumed that kids were to be seen, not heard. My parents were my parents, not my friends, and they never tried to be anything but a parent. They both loved me, but overt affection was not the custom in our house. Mother hugged me from time to time and Dad patted me on the head when he was pleased with something I did. For the most part, as long as I did my chores and stayed out of trouble, I was left alone and could do pretty much anything I wanted.

One difference between those days and today was that any adult could admonish a misbehaving kid and other parents expected them to do so when necessary. Parents knew one another better, working on similar jobs, going to church together, and living in the neighborhood. Adults quickly reported any misdeeds or misbehavior of any child to the responsible parents. While I hated punishment by my parents for something they knew I did, I felt worse if I got it for something another father or mother reported to them. Not only had I misbehaved, I had also embarrassed them.

In grade school, during warm weather, my friends and I usually went barefoot, but stopped once we entered junior high. Going barefoot all summer, we were apt to step on anything sharp and cut our feet. When I got a cut or stepped on a nail, Mom soaked my foot in kerosene. No one went to a doctor unless the injury was life-threatening. Iodine and "monkey blood" (mercurochrome) took care of most minor cuts. Sometimes an infection of an untreated cut or a scrape set in, causing red streaks to run up an arm or leg. Whenever Jean or I got an infection, Mother tied a poultice of raw bacon or a biscuit soaked in sweet milk onto the sore to draw out the poison.

For sore throats, she gave us a spoonful of sugar with a couple drops of kerosene or rubbed Vicks salve on our throats and up our noses. When we had a chest cold, Mother applied a mustard plaster to our chests, but watched carefully since a plaster caused blisters if it was left on the skin too long.

Twice a year Mother treated me for the "throughs" with doses of calomel—a Mercury compound used as a purgative then—each day for a week, followed by a last dose of a second strong laxative to clean my system. During that week of treatment, I could not exercise, swim, or eat dill or sour

An Unsung Hero: Coming of Age in the Dust Bowl

pickles—the acidity would cause me to salivate and raise sores in my mouth. The time of the "throughs" was a week of Hell for me, but I guess the treatment worked. I only remember going to the doctor's office twice as a boy. The doctor did see me two other times at home though—once when I had the German measles and a second time when a horse threw me and I landed on my head, knocking me out.

No one in my family usually went to the doctor's office when they were sick. When Dad returned to work on the railroad, he was required to take a physical exam. By Federal law, anyone under the age of fifty working for a railroad had to take an exam every two years; after 60, the exam was every year. The local Childress doctor charged Ft Worth & Denver a dollar for every physical exam including a urine test, listening to the patient's heart beats through his stethoscope, checking the mouth and throat, and feeling for ruptures. Of course, the doctor always asked the patient if he had any symptoms or thought something was wrong.

If someone was ill enough to see a doctor, he or she was usually too sick to get out of bed, so the doctor carried his little black physician's bag of examination tools and medicine and made a house call to the sick person. People in our neighborhood usually used home remedies rather than paying to see a doctor. If a prescription was necessary, Mother or Dad went to the drugstore where the pharmacist would pulverize bulk medicine with his mortar and pestle to make a powder to mix with water to drink. The pharmacist infrequently mixed liquid medicine himself. Vicks salve and castor oil were staples at our house. Some of the black kids wore asphidity bags around their necks to ward off disease—especially polio that was a common scare during the summers. I do not know what was in the asphidity bags, but the odor could clear your nostrils. None of my white school friends ever wore the bags, just black people.

During the Depression, the doctors in Childress took chickens, eggs, or home-canned vegetables as payment for treatment, since few of their patients had money. Doctors had to eat too, and few people had cash. If the sick had nothing to give them, the doctors usually provided their services free.

When we first moved to Childress, there was one hospital in town—a large two-story, wood-framed building located in the low-rent district and owned by our doctor. It had probably been a rooming house in its better days before the doctor bought it. A few years later, two other doctors built a second hospital of brick in a slightly better area of town. Hospital patients stayed in a ward with four to eight other people since there were no private or semi-private rooms available like today. Women gave birth in their homes—most of the time with the help of a midwife and, occasionally, a doctor.

Some physicians had offices downtown on the second or third floor of buildings where rent was cheaper. Their offices usually were two rooms, one for waiting and the second for examinations, and neither room had much furniture or equipment. In the examination room, furniture consisted of a chair for the doctor to sit and a single bed for patients to sit or lie down while he conducted his examination. Nurses, if any, also ran the waiting room and helped the doctor when needed. Our doctor's nurse was his wife.

Kids wore overalls and homemade shirts all through elementary school. In the summers, we exchanged the overalls for homemade shorts that buttoned up the front because zippers were expensive. I was almost 14 before pants with zippers became common. We went barefoot, not wearing shoes except for church. In the winters, most boys usually wore heavy coats, long underwear, and "aviator caps" with goggles for our eyes. My cap buttoned under my chin and covered my ears for wind protection. Some boys wore "boot-tees" because they laced up over your ankles and halfway up your calf. The best brands of boot-tees included a side pocket on one ankle where a boy could carry a pocketknife. Anyone who had a pair of those was the envy of all the boys in the neighborhood.

The girls bundled up in the winter too, but never wore pants, only dresses. They did not wear boots like boys, but slip-on, half-calved shoes. A few girls wore jodhpurs—a pair of trousers that flared at the hip and narrowed down below the knee to a tight cuff—in the winters. When the weather was rainy or snowy, the girls wore goulashes—rubber boots that fitted over their regular shoes—and took them off while at school.

I occasionally wore tennis shoes, but not frequently. The kind I had made my feet stink. In the summer, kids wore shoes to church or when we went with our parents to town. Regular shoes cost ninety-eight cents a pair, shirts about forty-nine cents each. Even as inexpensive as that sounds today, mothers and wives made most clothes for everyone in the family to save money, only buying overalls, a suit for men, and a single nice dress for women. Most people only had two or three changes of clothes, but they generally bathed only once a week, too. My dad was different; he took more baths than Jean and I combined.

5 Play Time

Every boy carried a sharp pocketknife, the handiest tool anyone could have and a necessity if you wanted to play "mumbley-peg"—no knife, no game. To play mumbley-peg, boys sat in a circle and attempted to replicate the previous boy's knife trick. For example, Bobby would balance his open knife with the tip of the blade on the end of his nose. Then, with a flick of the wrist of one hand, he tossed the knife—turning end over end—to stick the blade upright in the ground. If the knife failed to stick, he lost and the next boy did a different trick. If Bobby performed his trick successfully, the next thrower had to copy his trick exactly in order to stay in the game—the same throwing hand, starting position (nose, elbow, shoulder), and the same number of end over end revolutions. Consequently, most of us were pretty good at the game and throwing knives by the second or third grade.

We did all kinds of tricks chucking our knives in competition with one another—throwing to stick the point of the knife in trees, boards, or paper targets over different distances. We used pocketknives to cut sticks for bows, make notches for arrows, and carve our initials into a tree or park bench. There is no better feeling of accomplishment than getting a relatively straight branch from a willow tree, stripping off any small limbs, leaves, and bark before whittling the end into a sharp point to make a spear. Some guys were especially talented with their blades—able to carve small animals and such—but I never got that good.

Every boy carried his knife wherever he went—even to school. Everyone was expected to have a knife—man or boy—because it was so useful. Of course, my friends and I were forever cutting and accidentally stabbing ourselves—but never anyone else!

When I was in elementary school, I played baseball and football on vacant lots or in the street with the other boys in the neighborhood. We played baseball most of the year, then switched to football, as the weather got colder. I usually played on the vacant lot next door to our house since it was big enough for a baseball diamond or a good football field. I never saw a basketball backstop or anyone play the game of basketball until I got into junior high.

Baseball was a very popular Sunday afternoon sport in Childress and drew adults and children alike to the games, probably because the whole family could attend free. When I was seven or eight, Dad managed the railroad's team so we attended most of their games after church and lunch. Most of the adult teams had full uniforms with shirts, pants, hats, gloves, and spikes on their shoes. Some teams were so good they traveled to other towns for tournaments. My dad always had a friendly bet or two on the games even when he was the manager since he had played the game as a young man, knew most of the players on both teams, and considered himself a good judge of baseball talent.

As children, we played baseball in our regular clothes and usually barefooted. No one had a glove unless it was a worn-out, hand-me-down from an adult. Catching a hard hit or pitched fastball hurt when playing barehanded. If there was only one glove, no matter who owned it, the catcher used it because he had to catch every pitch. If there were two gloves, the catcher and the first baseman each got one. I do not recall ever playing a game when we had more than two gloves available for both teams.

We played our games with a baseball—called a "hardball"—because no one could afford to buy the bigger, mushy softball that girls and adults sometimes used. Our balls were always old ones—usually cast off from one of the adult baseball teams in town or caught when a home run flew over the fence in one of their games. We played with a ball even after we knocked its cover off by taping it together with black tar tape. There was usually only one or two bats—in as bad shape or worse than the baseballs—for both teams to use. If someone cracked a bat, we drove a nail through the bat perpendicular to the crack, bent the ends of the nail against the wood, and wrapped the repair with tape so that we could keep using it. I learned early to be sure the brand on the bat faced the sky during my swing so the bat would meet the ball with its stronger cross-grain surface.

We usually played "Scrub" because we never had enough guys to have two nine-man teams. As few as five or six people—a batter, catcher, pitcher, and others in the field—was enough to have a decent game. There were no strikes or balls in our games since we did not have an umpire and calling a strike always caused arguments. Anyway, the objective of the pitcher was to get the batter to hit the ball. If someone did not get a hit in the first four or five pitches, everyone yelled at the pitcher, "Let him hit!"

When the batter hit the ball, he had to run to first base, tag the base, and run back to home plate without being called out. Batters were out if the catcher got the ball and touched home plate before he returned. If the batter made it back, he made a score and got to bat again. If he was out, everyone moved up a position—the catcher became the batter, the pitcher the catcher, the infielder the pitcher, the outfielder the infielder, and the batter replaced the outfielder. Everyone was a one-man team and games lasted all afternoon until the running wore us out or it became too dark to see the ball.

When we played football, we usually had one ball—either something cheap the grass stickers we called "goat heads" easily punctured or a hand-me-down from the junior high or high school. Since we never had any equipment, we decided before beginning the game whether we would play touch or tackle. Even if we started playing touch, the game usually turned into tackle due to arguments whether the runner had been touched or not. In tackle, there is no dispute—the runner is either on the ground or not. I liked tackle best because I was strong and could drag one or two boys along until they jumped on my back and brought me down.

My favorite game was "Shinney"—played a lot like hockey, a game I discovered when I was older. Of course, we never played on ice in Childress. The simple game of Shinney required a tin can and sticks to knock the can between goal lines at each end of the field. The best cans were little Pet milk cans, but they were hard to come by, so we usually used old, mashed-up bean cans. Sticks were anything we found and could easily swing. When I knew we would play shinney, I ran home and got an old walking cane that I had found in someone's trash. The crook in the cane for the handle was larger than the end of most sticks so I had the odds on the other players. Shinney was hard on the shins because everyone would swing furiously at the can and hit other players' legs or feet when they missed; thus, the name "shinney."

Only boys played baseball, football, and shinney, but we did play other games with girls like hide-and-seek, Red Rover, May I, London Bridge is Falling Down, Annie Come Over, and others that we made up. Peggy, a tow-headed girl with glasses who lived two doors down, taught me to play

William M. Forsythe

hopscotch and jacks. Girls jumped rope—sometimes by themselves with their own rope and sometimes with a long rope tied to a tree with one girl swinging the rope while two or three other girls jumped at the same time. At school recess, girls usually jumped rope the whole period while the boys played baseball and football.

I loved to roller skate on sidewalks. Bobby, my best friend, and I skated everywhere in town where there was a hard surface. For many years, my only present for Christmas was a pair of roller skates—sometimes even when Mom and Dad could not afford them. A skate consisted of two adjustable steel platforms, four steel wheels, and clamps to attach the skate to a shoe, which tightened with a skate key. I always carried the skate key with me because one of the skates often uncoupled from my shoes. As the skates wore out, the clamps loosened and needed retightening repeatedly. I usually wore my skates down to their wheel rims by August each year. Then I would take them apart and make a scooter so I could scooter if not skate.

After I got the hang of it, riding a scooter was easy. You put one foot on the scooter, held on to the handlebars, and pushed with your free foot. There were no hills in Childress, but whenever I found a slope where gravity would let me ride without pushing, I put both feet on the scooter and coasted as far as I could. Although not fast, scootering was better than walking.

Making a scooter was not much harder than riding one. After finding a two-by-four about five to six feet long, I cut it in half and nailed the two pieces together to form an "L" shape. I also nailed a couple of braces on each side of the L joint to strengthen the connection. Then, I separated the two parts of a skate—each with two wheels. I nailed one piece to the front part near the "L" of the bottom board and the second piece to the back part. Then I nailed a small piece of wood across the top of the vertical board for handlebars and was ready to rumble.

I liked to walk on stilts, but I usually had to make them first. Making stilts was harder than making skates since stilts required two long pieces of board and we did not have the money to buy anything. For decent height stilts, I needed two two-by-four inch boards at least five feet long and a third shorter piece. Once I found the wood in an alley or down at the railroad yards, I collected some two-inch nails, an old belt, and got out Dad's saw and hammer. I cut the shorter two-by-four into two six-inch long blocks slanted at one end in a forty-five degree angle. When the short blocks were ready, I nailed each block to one of the long boards, usually about three to four feet from the end. The height of the stilts depended upon the lengths of the longer two-by-fours. After cutting the belt into straps, I nailed one end of the strap to the block and the other end to the stilt, making a stirrup to keep my foot from slipping off the block while walking on the stilts. My last step was to whittle the top ends of the two stilts to fit my hands. I eventually got my stilts so high that I had to climb on top of the fence next to our house to reach the stirrups. I learned to walk on much shorter stilts and made them higher as I got older. I usually kept my old stilts around for Jean to use or for when I needed practice.

While stilts were fun, they were not very practical if I had to walk a long distance. In those cases, my friends and I wore "Tom Walkers," empty oil cans on the bottom of our feet. Years ago, most people bought motor oil pumped from a bulk tank at the gas stations for their car. However, there were some people affluent enough to buy oil in tin cans. When they changed the oil, they discarded the cans in their trash—our treasure chests that we checked a couple of times a week looking for anything we might use.

When I found a couple of empty oil cans, I punched a hole in each end, then strung a long piece of wire through the holes with a loop on each end that I held in my hand. Holding the loops—two loops in each hand—I pulled the cans tight against my feet and walked. If I wore shoes, I did not need the holes and loops. Laying each can on its side, I stomped the can in the middle to bend the ends around the sides of my shoe like a roller skate clamp. If I was lucky, I could walk all the way to the store on the oilcans, clanging and banging the whole trip. Oh, what fun!

Sometimes, my friends and I went down to the train depot and repair yards. We knew most of the men working there since, like Dad, my friends' fathers worked for the railroad. Our parents did not like us playing around the tracks because of the danger, but big, noisy, dirty equipment was too attractive for most boys to heed their parents' instructions.

Broken bits of metal or discarded wood that we could use to make things was always ours for the taking and watching the switch engines shunt boxcars around the tracks was fun. The huge brick roundhouse was usually full of big locomotives in various stages of repair. Freight and passenger trains steamed in and out of town several times a day; the latter stopped at the depot to let passengers on and off. Whenever a train passed us as we walked beside the tracks, the engineer would blow the steam whistle and wave to us and the brakeman and conductor sitting in the caboose would lean out of the cupola to yell "Hello." By the time I was nine or ten, we quit going down to the tracks because the novelty had worn off, but it was a great adventure the first four and five years I lived in Childress.

An Unsung Hero: Coming of Age in the Dust Bowl

Sometimes, when someone had a spare penny, we put it on the rail for the train to mash it flat. A squashed penny usually had an unusual shape with edges as thin as notebook paper. After the train passed, we searched the ground around the rails to find the penny that sometimes stuck to a train wheel for a short distance before falling off. When we found the flattened penny, we punched a hole in the thinnest part with our pocketknives, ran a string through the hole, and wore the penny around our necks like a medal. Every son of a railroad man had one of those pennies around their neck. Other kids traded their treasures with a railroad kid for the pennies.

The kids in my neighborhood played outside until supper and then again afterwards until bedtime. There was nothing to do in the house since few families owned a radio and the electric lights did not emit enough light to read. Back in those days, the radio and movies were the only way that we received national and world news. Newspapers carried mostly local news and a few national stories, but nothing like today. After supper, most families went outside to sit on the front porch and chat. There were always other neighbors on their porches, so families visited almost every evening. The other children and I liked to listen to the stories the adults told. However, any time the stories began to get interesting, Mother or Dad would always say, "You kids, go on off and play."

6 Ghosts, Witches & Circuses

Even though we played outside until called for bed, I never conquered my fear of the dark. I found ways to handle my terror, though. Sometimes a group of us went in the vacant lot next door, sat down, and told ghost stories. Afterwards, we were too scared to walk home alone, even when only two or three houses away from the lot. Although there were no streetlights in our neighborhood, the bushes and trees cast long shadows that jumped and trembled in the wind from moonlight or the occasional light from someone's front room. Hidden feral cats and dogs, along with a hungry raccoon or coyote, made rustling sounds as they foraged in the unlit yards and alleys. To ensure everyone got home safely, we all walked to the first kid's home, dropped him off, then walked to the next house, etc. Everything was okay unless I was the last one with no one to accompany me to my house. That is when I found out how fast I could run!

Bobby and I spent every day together. We were fearless except for ghosts, vampires, haunted houses, and the dark. Every kid knew that vacant houses were haunted and everyone was afraid to go in one. We ran by them as fast as possible, especially after the sun went down and evil creatures came out to play.

The most direct way to or from town meant walking by an old, dilapidated two-story house abandoned years before. The older kids told us a murder and suicide followed by a haunting, was the reason the house remained vacant. Each window held broken panes of glass and the ceiling of the porch across the front of the house sagged badly in one corner where a column had rotted away. Wooden shingles, blown off the roof, lay in the front yard amidst the weeds and other debris that had collected over the years. The paint had long ago disappeared, exposing brown, weathered boards to the elements.

We knew it was haunted. The front door swung opened and closed whenever the wind blew as if to invite unsuspecting children inside for fun and games. Everybody knew the ghosts were responsible. Bobby and I always dared each other to go inside, walk up the stairs, and look out the front window of the second floor to prove our bravery, knowing a ghost was waiting to snatch anyone dumb enough to walk through the door. We had learned all about ghosts from older kids telling stories on the vacant lot. I don't think either one of us took up the dare until we were at least ten years old and then only in the daylight.

Childress had several witches. While we skated, I often saw one walking downtown or on a sidewalk. My friends said she always carried a straight razor in her shirt pocket. She had long grey hair, framed by huge, round ear lobes—almost as large as golf balls—and bushy black, unkempt eyebrows. While it was safe to look at her if you were far away, everyone knew to look away when you got close. You never looked her in the eye because she might remember and pay you a visit. Whenever I got too close, I could feel her looking at me with her evil eye and hear her muttering as I passed by. I was afraid she was putting a curse on me. I never spoke to her, but walked by as fast as I could whenever I saw her. All of the kids knew that she caused any bad luck that happened to us.

Even with our fears, Halloween was always a fun time even though we did not trick-or-treat as kids do now. During the Depression, people did not have the money to buy treats for children or fancy costumes for them to wear. Most of the

Halloween activities took place at our grade school. Of course, during the week before, the teachers would always read some scary story like Washington Irving's "The Legend of Sleepy Hollow" or "Rip Van Winkle" to set the right mood for the event.

On Halloween, our grade school always had a school fair for entertainment. Each room sponsored a different game—throwing darts at balloons, bobbing for apples, or a cakewalk—where every child could play at no cost. When we tired of the games, my friends and I would go outside to stick potatoes in the exhaust pipes of the older cars, then hide and watch when the owners came outside and tried to start the car. A car would not start with a plugged exhaust pipe. The potato in the tailpipe kept exhaust gases from leaving the engine's cylinders so new gas vapors could not get in. In other words, a car with a potato up the exhaust could not breathe! We lay on the ground hidden from view as the driver cranked his car without success, usually cursing a blue streak until someone pointed out the potato in the exhaust pipe. The driver got out, yelled into the dark—not seeing us but knowing we were there—and removed the potato. Sometimes he threw it wherever he thought we might be hiding. This trick only worked once or twice each Halloween because people leaving later in the evening checked their exhaust pipes for potatoes before trying to start their cars.

Older boys used watermelon rinds instead of potatoes for their fun. After setting a watch to warn them if someone came out, two or three teenagers would lift the back of a parked Model-T and set one of the wheels on a watermelon rind. When the owner left the school to go home, the old T just sat with one of its rear wheel spinning on the slick rind as the car was too light-weight to move. When the driver figured out that the wheel was spinning, even though the car was not moving, he would get out and find the rind. Since he could not lift the wheel off the rind by himself, he had to find someone to help. Sometimes, the more stubborn drivers would keep spinning the wheel until the tire wore through the softer rind and gained traction. Our pranks did not hurt anyone or do any damage except for the driver's inconvenience and ego. After all, it was Halloween when everyone knew the ghostly spirits were active.

Once each year, Heganbech, Wallace, Forepaw, and Sells Brothers—the second largest circus in the USA—arrived in Childress early on a spring morning, their pending arrival announced by colorful posters and signboards distributed by their advance men the prior week. Knowing the circus was coming to town, all of my friends agreed, "to heck with school." We arrived at the train station by 5:30 AM the day the circus train pulled into town, hoping to work in exchange for a ticket into the Matinee. The cost of admission was a quarter, but who wanted to pay when you could work your way in?

Besides, quarters were very scarce in the 1930s, especially for kids. A quarter would buy five cokes or five hamburgers. Banana splits were only fifteen cents. A quarter would pay for two movie admissions with enough money left to buy a bag of popcorn. An adult could ride a cab to anywhere in town and return home and have enough change to buy a bag of Bull Durham tobacco. In the summer, a quarter paid for Bobby and me to go to the swimming pool and buy a big candy bar to share when we walked home. A quarter was a lot of money with plenty of choices about where to spend it.

When the circus train stopped downtown, the animals, tents, and all of the other paraphernalia required to stage the show had to be unloaded and moved ten blocks to the fairgrounds. The elephants pulled the heavy wagons with the poles, tents, and seats while horses and ponies pulled the animal cages and the smaller equipment. The Heganbech circus had at least twenty-five elephants. Since there were no zoos in our area, no television, and few movie theaters, going to the circus gave kids and some adults the opportunity to see a live elephant for the first time, to say nothing about the lions, camels, and other exotic animals. Hardly anyone had ever seen as many wild animals in one place at the same time. Small towns did not have animal parks or zoos and people generally did not travel far from their hometowns to bigger cities prior to World War II.

As soon as the first circus wagons arrived at the fairgrounds, the boys and young men began pestering the circus people for jobs and passes. Carrying water for the animals was the best job, but none of the jobs were especially hard. Running errands was a good job too, but that meant losing the chance to watch the elephants and camels drink.

Some of the larger boys drove the stakes and helped the circus roustabouts raise the Big Top. It was always a thrill to see the huge tent go up. Then up went the seats for the patrons along with the three rings where the action took place. When the work was done, everyone headed home to await the parade the next day.

At noon on the day of the show, the circus parade started at the fairgrounds, went up the length of Main Street to the train depot, and returned down Commerce Street to the fairgrounds. The procession always began with two lines of elephants marching side-by-side, accompanied by clowns on unicycles and little tricycles carrying bright red and blue balloons beside each line. Except for the two leaders, each elephant held the tail of the elephant in front with his trunk.

An Unsung Hero: Coming of Age in the Dust Bowl

The Big Show always started at two o'clock the same afternoon.

The circus was great, but it only came once a year. I thought carnivals were even more fun because they usually came twice a year—in the spring and fall. About two weeks before the carnival was scheduled to open, posters appeared in store windows and on the buildings downtown. The kids in the county were more than ready when the show finally arrived. The first on my list of things to do at the carnival was the rides, but I also looked forward, almost as much, to cotton candy, the different sideshows, and the prospect of winning at pitching pennies.

Carnivals and circuses were the only times we got to eat cotton candy. Even though you could buy them at the local café any time, hot dogs were a lot better at the carnival too. We did not have fast-food restaurants like McDonalds or BurgerKing in those days. If someone wanted a hot dog, he walked in and sat down in a regular cafe, ordered from the menu, and waited for the wiener to cook before he ate. While hot dogs were a nickel at either place, there was no waiting at the carnival or circus for the dog to cook.

One of the tricks the carnival people played on townspeople was for the carny to paint the index or middle finger of his hand the same pinkish color as a boiled hot dog, then craftily lay that finger in the bun so it looked like a hotdog in the bun as he put mustard and onions on top. When the carny handed the buyer the bun, he would slip his finger out so that the customer was left with just a bun with mustard and onions. If the customer said, "I don't have a weenie," the vendor pointed to one on the ground and said, "You dropped it." Boiled wieners were always on the ground around hotdog stands. The carnival people did not do the trick every time. I guess, they only picked people who were less likely to make a big fuss. I never saw one of them try to pull that trick on a kid.

For thirty cents, I could have a great time—go on a couple of rides, see a sideshow or two, pitch some pennies, and finally eat cotton candy. The sideshows were terrific. Where else could I see a fat lady, a leopard man with tattoos covering his body, a bearded lady, or a wild man who would bite the head off of a live chicken? That didn't include the snake charmer in a pen full of live snakes, the sword swallower, the fire-eater, the alligator man, a two-headed calf, and a real live hermaphrodite. All of the exhibits for just the cost of a dime!

When the main sideshow was over, another barker called people to watch the hoochie-goochie show, advertised by scantily dressed girls in grass skirts and halter-tops who danced on a stage in front of the tent. I never saw anybody move like those girls did in those skirts, but my friends and I were always too young to go inside and see the show. We did get to pitch pennies at a board with the chance to win if one of our pennies landed in a numbered square without touching another square. The square in the middle of the board paid a quarter if a penny landed there. There were also wheels of fortune for adults to spin and win fifty dollars if the marker landed on the right number. At another game, the carnival man would hide a peanut under one of three walnut shells and then move the three shells around to hide which one hid the peanut. For a cost of fifty cents, adults tried to pick the shell covering the peanut. If they picked correctly, they won a dollar. I noticed they were wrong many more times than they were correct. In those days of carnivals, there were more gambling games for grownups than games kids could play.

I liked going to the fun house where I could see water run up-hill and my reflection in different kinds of mirrors that

An Unsung Hero: Coming of Age in the Dust Bowl

made me tall, short, fat, skinny, or distorted. The fun house had two places where air would blow up women's dresses and show their legs when they walked over it; sometimes, the skirts were blown waist high so there were always a lot of young men and teenagers hanging around. Everybody just laughed, even the girls whose dresses blew high. "How do you suppose people would react to that trick today?" I wonder.

The carnival had fellows who guessed a person's weight and age for a penny. If guessed incorrectly, the patron won a small prize. There was always a fortuneteller or two, but none of us kids tried that. One year, the carnival had a boxer who dared anyone to fight him for a one hundred dollar prize going to the winner. I do not know how many tried for the hundred dollars, but some did.

Going to the carnival was fun because it was live with attractions that I could reach out and touch. Carnivals today with all the quirks and games may seem commonplace, but they brought lots of excitement to my friends and me growing up in Childress.

While the arrival of a circus or a carnival was a great day for most people—some of our neighbors in Childress, people living in the smaller communities around the town, and many farmers—could not afford the expense to go. Tickets for four children cost as much as a day's earnings from working in the fields. For those who did not have a job, it cost a fortune. It is hard to imagine today how far it was between "pleasure quarters" in the days of the Great Depression.

William M. Forsythe

7 Rubber Guns and Night Games

My friends and I spent a lot of time looking for lead metal. When we found it, we melted the lead in a tin can. Some brick companies made bricks with a five-point star inlay as part of their name. We would find a brick with the star inlay, pour the hot lead in the inlay, and add a big safety pin before the lead cooled. The result: a five-pointed star just like a sheriff's badge.

We also made skullcaps by taking our fathers' old felt fedora hats and cutting off the brims. Most of the time, a kid had to fold up the edges inside to made the hat fit since adults' heads were bigger. We decorated the hats and sometimes our shirts with soda pop lids. Being careful to keep the layer intact, we pried the cork out of the inside of the bottle cap with our pocket knives, put the tin side of the cap on the outside of our felt hats, the cork layer on the inside, and pressed the two together to attach the bottle caps to the hats.

If we had a badge, we had to have a gun. Fortunately in the days of yore, apples, oranges, lemons, and other fruit came in wooden boxes about thirty-six inches long and sixteen inches deep and wide. The ends were solid pieces of 1-inch white pine—a soft wood—with sides, top, and bottom of thin slats. The downtown stores gave us the boxes whenever we asked, realizing we made most of our toys out of the boxes.

The box ends were long enough to make rubber gun pistols and, if careful, I could get about three pistols out of each end. Pistols were about sixteen inches long due to the size of the apple box ends. Using Dad's ripsaw, I cut the end into shapes that looked like pistols with long barrels, offsetting the handle a little to make the gun easier to hold. I attached a wooden clothespin to the handle, looping a rubber band round and round until the clothespin was secure. The clothespin was the trigger of the gun so I used as many loops as possible to make it harder to open the clothespin by mistake, thus avoiding misfires.

I loaded my gun by placing one end of a folded rubber band in the clothespin and stretching the other end to fit around the end of the barrel. When I opened the clothespin, the rubber band would fly from the gun in the general direction where I pointed. With most guns, I had one shot. If I wanted a two-shot pistol, I looped another band around the whole gun atop the first band and shot by rolling the top band off with my thumb.

Ammunition for all the guns was the same—strips of old rubber auto tire inner tubes six to eight inches round. Most kids tried to keep any inner tubes they found for a source of ammunition when they needed it. Boys who did not keep their families' old inner tubes or who ran out of bands had to search the filling stations for old inner tubes—not very common even though most service stations would give them to you if they had any. Using our pocketknives, we cut the inner tubes into three-quarter-inch wide bands to make ammo. Every boy I knew made his own guns, not because our parents would not help us, but because we never asked. Parents were generally working all of the time trying to feed their families; and anyway, making your own gun was part of the fun.

When I wanted a longer gun—a rifle or a machine gun that we called a "tommy gun"—I had to find a longer piece of wood. My friends and I usually walked up and down the alleys looking at stuff people threw away for something interesting. If we were lucky, we found discarded wood good enough to make some stilts or a rifle. Rubber gun rifles were about four feet long, sawed in the shape of a rifle with notches cut about half way down the end of the barrel. I made a notch by sawing perpendicular to the barrel and a second, sloping cut toward the first cut. Clothespins were not necessary for rifles or Tommy guns since the inner tube bands stretched from the end of the gun into each notch. I always loaded the gun from the end farthest away from the end of the barrel first so every shot counted. When I wanted to fire, I just rolled the stretched band out of the notch with my thumb. A rifle usually had seven to twelve notches with as many shots as notches in the barrel.

Tommy guns resembled rifles, except for a second handle about halfway up the barrel. I cut the same kind of notches, but more; tommy guns had ten to fifteen shots. The big difference between a Tommy gun and a rifle was the different trigger, a long string attached to the barrel of a Tommy gun with a tack. When I loaded the gun, the string went in the notches under the bands. When I pulled the string, I could fire one Band, or as many as I wanted at once.

Finally, I always carried a "safety" in my pocket or stuck one in my belt under my shirt out of sight. The safety was a small pistol loaded with bands made from bicycle tire inner tubes. Bicycle inner tubes were harder to find because their owners kept patching them and the patched parts of the tube were too stiff for ammo. When I did not have bicycle bands, I had to tie knots in the larger auto inner tube bands to make them shorter, but shortened bands did not work as well. That was too bad since the safety was very important—it could save your life when the ammo ran out for the other weapons.

In addition to all of our loaded guns, we carried another forty or fifty extra bands as spare ammo on an old belt that went over our shoulders. When I put on my belt, I was loaded for the war that raged all over our neighborhood. Being shot with one of the bands hurt if you were close to the shooter, so we tried never to hit anyone in the face or head. I always tried to remember to pick up any bands I found, especially ones for my safety, and take them home to be ready for the next war. However, sometimes I had to go home before I was finished. One of our rules was that any band that had been shot was the property of whoever found it. By the time I entered junior high, we quit playing with rubber guns.

However, our fun did not end when the sun went down. There were few cars in Childress and even fewer out at night. All of the automobiles had poor headlights; they were more like house lamps that scattered light into the sky as well as the road ahead—the focused sealed beams on cars today illuminates the road much better. If we saw a car coming after dark, half of us, boys and girls, would run to one side of the street and half to the other side. When the car got close, we would act as if we were pulling a rope between the two groups, stretched across the street as tight as we could pull. With those old lights, the driver could not see whether we held a real or imaginary rope so he would hit the brake pedals as hard as he could push. As soon as he stopped, all of the kids would run away and the driver would discover it was just a trick.

Sometimes at night, the boys went "tic-tacking." Girls never went, since getting caught could have repercussions at home. Tic-tacking required a spool of thread or twine, a safety pin, and a wet rag. We tied one end of the thread to the safety pin, slipped up to a window of a dark room and hooked the safety pin in the window screen, and then sneaked away while unrolling the thread off the spool. When we got about thirty or forty feet from the window, we pulled the thread tight and started rubbing it with the wet rag. Rubbing the thread made an awful sound, and the wire screens carried the noise right through the window into the house. To anyone inside, the noise sounded like someone was tearing the window out. When the light came on or someone came outside, we dropped the thread and ran like crazy. When you played outside after dark, you had to find something to do.

Our safety, day or night, was never a problem or something that caused parents' worry. Even though we went everywhere in the neighborhood, we were nearly always in pairs or bigger groups. We walked to and from school in cliques. We also walked up and back from town; it was only nine blocks.

Parents did not worry about the where-abouts of their kids because everyone was active outside their houses, except in the winter months. During the day, women hung clothes on outside lines to dry, beat rugs, or swept off porches throughout the town. Men repaired old cars or worked around their houses fixing things. The windows and doors of every house were open so even those inside could hear a yell or scream and come running.

In the summers to keep cool, people slept on their screened-in back porch if they had one, or outside in the yard. They simply moved their beds out and slept without fear. Most of the women got up and went in the house just before daylight. We did not have a back porch, but we slept out a lot. It was not bad, maybe a little gritty when the sand blew, but a heck of a lot cooler than being indoors.

8 The Weekends

When I was in elementary school, I always looked forward to the weekend. Saturday was the best day of the week and, most of the time, the whole day belonged to kids. The streets downtown filled with people coming to town from farms and ranches to shop and see friends. People from the country rode horses or came to town in a wagon and team. There were places for the teams to park between Main and Commerce streets and a wagon yard just one block west of Main Street. When those spaces filled, you could not find a parking place less than two blocks from the commercial district. Men dressed in overalls, women in long dresses, and children walked shoulder-to-shoulder down the sidewalks and spilled into the street, sometimes stopping to greet and shake hands. There was always a hellfire-and-brimstone preacher on one corner, shaking his Bible in one hand and prophesying that if people did not change their ways, God was coming to end the world and bringing the Four Horsemen of the Apocalypse—War, Famine, Death, and Christ—to judge the wicked and the dead. The town was alive until nine o'clock at night on Saturdays.

Saturdays was also the day for getting a haircut if you could afford it. Most kids, including me, had their hair cut by their mother at the kitchen table. Many men, especially farmers, didn't shave during the week, but got shaved by the barber on Saturday. I never missed a chance to go with Dad when he got a haircut or shave on Saturday. It was an experience just listening to the stories told by the customers in the shop.

There were two barbershops in Childress, one with three chairs and the other with two as I remember. Haircuts cost a quarter and shaves cost fifteen cents. Both shops would be full with men waiting and gossiping about one thing or another— mostly the goings-on in Washington, the weather, or the high school football team. There was no cussing allowed in the barbershop. Life was tough, but men had respect for kids and women. Using the word "damn" or "hell" could get a customer thrown out of a place of business.

Watching a barber shave someone was a picture of indulgence for the one being shaved and an exhibition of great skill by the shaver. The barber kept hot towels in a steamer by the stove. As the customer reclined in the barber chair, the barber carefully wrapped a hot towel over and around his face. As the towel cooled, the barber took an ivory-handled shave brush of badger hair and stirred up a cup of thick white foam—the shaving cream. When the foam was ready, he removed the hot towel and spread foam all over the lower part of the waiting face—talking without pause as he carefully brushed the foam around the nose and ears of his customer.

As the foam softened the bristly whiskers, the barber opened his straight razor—a thin piece of steel so sharp it could cut paper by touch—and began to hone the blade on the leather strop hanging beside the chair. When the blade reached the point of perfection only known to the barber, he put one hand on the waiting man's head and took quick, short strokes down each cheek, wiping the foam and the shorn whiskers on a towel slung over his shoulder.

Dad's barber used to hold him by the nose when he shaved Dad's upper lip. I suppose that was to keep from cutting his lips or nose if Dad moved. Watching the barber shave a neck—the most dangerous part of the procedure—

fascinated me. Dad stretched his head back, trusting his throat to the ministrations of the barber. One slip and the razor could slash his neck from ear to ear. My friends and I never tired of watching the barber shave someone—not wanting to miss seeing someone's throat cut.

When the haircut, shave, or both were finished, the barber splashed lotion on his hands and patted Dad's face and dusted talcum powder on his neck. When he stood up, the shine boy brushed any hair off Dad's clothes. A man felt like a million dollars after a haircut and shave, whether he was out of a work or the town banker.

Saturday was also movie day for those who had the money. Usually a couple of boys from the neighborhood who had collected bottles or done chores for a little money during the week before were the ones with the money to go. When we got up on a Saturday morning, we walked downtown, stopping by the haunted house to see if a murder had occurred overnight (it never did), and then went on to the jails and fire station by City Hall.

Childress had two fire trucks and a couple of full-time firemen who slept on the second floor of the fire station. When the firemen got an alarm, they slid down a big brass pole from their room to the fire trucks. Sometimes, they let me and the other boys slide down the pole. It was a long reach to grab the pole and a little scary, but quite an adventure when you are ten years old. The firemen always had a friendly dog eager for petting.

The City Jail was just two cells in City Hall, each having a window with black steel bars in the back brick wall. The front of each cell had bars with a door of bars and a lock. Between the two cells, a third set of bars stretched from the ceiling to the floor so prisoners could reach into the other cell

William M. Forsythe

if they wanted. The steel bars were far enough apart that an arm could be extended, but too narrow for a body unless the prisoner was really, really skinny. I never heard of anyone escaping through the bars.

Crime was not much of a problem in Childress in the early 1930s, so the prisoners were mostly drunks and vagrants. The police knew everyone who might steal, bootleg, gamble, or make trouble but were rarely called upon to arrest anyone. Most people left the doors and windows of their houses unlocked and open unless it was cold and even then, any stranger could open the door and walk right in. If anyone lost their key or found a locked door, the hardware store would sell them a skeleton key that could open most of the locks in town.

In the 1930s, the police could put someone in jail for three days for vagrancy if he did not have a job. The lawmen didn't bother the people who lived in Childress since quite a few, like Dad, were out of work frequently. The vagrancy laws applied mostly to the hoboes who rode in on freight trains and stayed too long. The town's citizens were uncomfortable with strangers who did not have a place to live, panhandled for food, and stayed past their welcome.

When we visited the city jail, we did not actually go back to the cells, but looked at them from the hall. We never recognized any of the prisoners either, but we always hoped to see someone like Machine Kelley or BabyFace Nelson whose pictures were in the post office and rumored to pass through our part of Texas from time to time.

The County Jail was a building next to the County Courthouse. The sheriff lived downstairs and kept his prisoners upstairs. Most prisoners in the County Jail had been arrested for bootlegging. The sheriff did not allow kids to go inside the county jail, but sometimes prisoners would holler at us from the second floor cell windows and we might talk a few minutes. Mostly, the prisoners asked for cigarettes, but none of us smoked and did not have any to give them. Anyway, there was not a way to get a cigarette to them on the second floor; throwing a single cigarette in any kind of wind and hitting where you intended to hit is impossible because a cigarette is so light.

When our civic duties were over, we checked out the alleys to see if we could find anything useful before the movie opened. If we found anything we wanted to take home, it had to be small enough to carry into the theatre or we had to find a place to hide it while we were inside. Except for stuff that had your name carved on it or burned into a surface where people could see it, all boys operated under the "finders, keepers" rule. The guys with you wouldn't try to claim your find after you hid it; it was other boys looking for treasure while you were in the movie that you had to worry about.

As soon as the movie opened, we went in, usually finding some other boys to sit with. The theatre, like the other Childress buildings, did not have air-conditioning. To circulate the air, especially in the hot summers, the manager left the back and front doors open. When a dust storm blew in, the air inside wasn't too bad because the sand usually blew through fast. Although there were occasions when we could not see the screen clearly, we always stayed and got our dime's worth by watching the movie at least twice. Who would leave because of a little dust when you have an opportunity to see the movie feature, a newsreel, comedy or cartoon, and a chapter of a serial like *Flash Gordon* or *King of the Wild*?

On the Saturdays when we didn't have the money for the movie, we filled a pocket full of rocks; took our slingshots, a sandwich, a stick and walked to a canyon close to the old

William M. Forsythe

Goodnight-Loving Cattle Trail about three miles outside of town. We spent the day shooting at rabbits or birds—which we never hit—and running up and down the canyon or climbing on the rocks. If it were warm, we took our bathing suits just in case we wanted to swim in one of the cattle tanks. I always carried a stick in case I found a can I could knock ahead as I walked. Kicking a can or hitting it while walking seemed to speed any walk; before I knew it, I was at my destination.

Sometimes, we walked about two and a half miles to the old city lake where my pals and I spent the day swimming, fishing, or just throwing rocks. Sometimes, we met other guys there—but whether or not we met anyone else, it was a day of fun. Our tails drug all the way home and we were starved when supper was ready.

Saturdays had their downside too. Everyone bathed on Saturday night and nearly everyone in our neighborhood went to church on Sunday. It was as regular as going to school.

We went to church every Sunday—rain, sunshine, windy, or cold. All of the men wore hats—which they removed before going inside—suits with a vest, white shirts, and ties. The churches lacked cooling and the Church of Christ where we attended had no ceiling fans. A local funeral home furnished paper fans on a stick that the ushers passed out at the door. To be able to stand the heat, everyone fanned and fanned—mothers and dads using a wrist flick while kids used their whole arms. Even so, I was always hot and sweaty.

Dad always shined his only pair of black dress shoes the night before Church. Usually in his undershirt, sometimes still wearing his regular fedora perched on the crown of his head, and smoking a pipe, he sat on a kitchen table chair with a Kiwi tin of paste, some rags, and a couple of wooden-handled shoe brushes of horsehair. One brush was stiffer than the other; the softer one used for buffing.

After removing the shoelaces and knocking off the dust and any mud from both shoes, he picked one—always the left shoe for some unknown reason—and carefully wiped a damp cloth over the leather surface, paying particular attention to the intersection of the upper shoe body and the sole. He cleaned a little bit, then held the shoe up to his face for inspection to be sure he hadn't missed a little speck which might cause the polish to smear when he applied it. When the left shoe was finished, he repeated the same process with the right one, being careful to tamp his pipe if necessary.

Using another rag, he dipped two fingers of his right hand into the open tin of polish and smoothly applied the paste to his left shoe—now dry from his earlier ministrations—held in his left hand. The right shoe dried while he worked on the left. Dad rubbed his fingers in little circles, carefully applying the paste as evenly as possible, starting with the toe of the shoe, then the sides, the tongue, and finally the back. As he did during the cleaning of the shoe, he constantly lifted it to his eyes while polishing—turning it this way and that—to ensure the paste was perfect. When he was satisfied with the quality of his work, he carefully placed the polished shoe on the ground, sat up and stretched his arms above his head, relit his pipe, and started on the right shoe.

When he was sure the polish on the left shoe was dry, he stroked each side of the shoe with the stiff-bristled brush, swishing back and forth across the length of the shoe to a staccato rhythm. When he finished the sides, he moved to the toe, then the top where the exposed tongue waited, and finally, the back of the shoe—his only adjustment being the length of the to-and-fro brush strokes. When the job was up to par, he repeated the same procedure on the remaining shoe.

For most people, the result at that point may have been enough, but Dad was just getting started. He picked up each shoe again, and using the softer bristle brush, caressed its surface in soft, short pats as if expecting the shoe to blush with color. If he did not achieve the shine he sought, he would spit softly on the offending spot and re-apply his buffing efforts. By the time he finished, the shoes gleamed in the kitchen light, looking almost new.

When I was eight and had my first good pair of shoes, Dad expected me to join him in the kitchen, preparing my own shoes. Since I regularly outgrew my shoes every six months, I never developed the attachment to them that Dad developed for his footwear. In addition, Mother expected me to take a bath and go to bed after shoe shining, so I never looked forward to our shoe-shining sessions. Focused on his own handiwork, Dad did not talk much to me as he ministered to his shoes, except to admonish me when he thought I was derelict in my effort.

I learned a lot about Hell at a young age going to church. Mother always made sure that Jean and I went to Sunday school before Church where we heard Bible stories and talked about what Heaven was like. After Sunday school, we joined Mother and Dad in our regular seats—a straight-backed oak pew on the left side of the center aisle halfway between the front door and the communion table—for every service. Dad always sat on the end of the pew next to the center aisle, Mother next to him, then Jean, then me. When I was lucky, another family with a boy who I knew would sit next to us, the boy beside me and his father the farthest away.

The Church of Christ does not believe in musical instruments in church, so different male members led us in opening songs and prayer before the preacher delivered his sermon. Our preacher, Brother Grey, was a tall, thin man with a puckered mouth as if he ate persimmons all of the time. He owned a farm outside of town where he spent most of the week. He and his wife had three girls at least five years older than me; his wife was short and heavy, but the girls were as thin and long-limbed as he was.

When Brother Grey preached, his sharp nasal voice stabbed the air and punctured the guilty hearts of any sinners who might have been tempted to sleep in the heat. Brother Grey never smiled during a sermon, but paced back and forth in the front of the church with his arms flailing at the invisible sins accompanying the church members while he held forth about the Devil's temptations and the promise that each of us would burn in Hell unless we confessed and repented our individual trespasses. He said, "God wants you to be good, to follow his commandments, but Man is a natural sinner and turns his back on his Savior." His sermons were full of Bible verses that he repeated from memory, bludgeoning home his message, verse after verse, as he roamed up and down the center aisle for emphasis, looked each person in their eye as if knowing that they had sinned during the week and would surely go to Hell.

The preacher described the Fire that would burn for eternity without consuming flesh, and the pain and the loneliness we could expect if we did not change our ways and accept Jesus Christ as our Savior. I learned that a hummingbird, carrying a single grain of sand in its beak and flying to the moon and back every 1000 years, could move the whole earth—one sand grain at a time—to the moon before one second passed in Eternity. Brother Grey ended every sermon with the scripture of John 3:16, "For God so loved the world that he gave his one and only son, that whoever believes of him shall not perish but have eternal life." He stretched out his arms and widely smiled, inviting sinners to join him in the front of the church. Usually, four or five audience members responded to the Invitation, women crying and men with tears flowing down their cheeks as they walked to the front of the church for baptism or to repent publicly for their personal failures. The whole church rejoiced with song and prayed with the sinners, thanking God they had been saved—at least for that moment in time.

Brother Grey and other preachers like him—with their sermons of hell and brimstone—kept me aware of my sins, but they also taught me about love, giving, and duty to one another. I always left church resolved to be a better person. Life seemed so simple in those days, so black and white; we believed in the Bible's Ten Commandments, family, patriotism, and honor. I was taught to never tell a lie, never to hit a girl, and that when I gave my word, it was a bond never to be broken, no matter how difficult the circumstances.

After Church, my family walked home for a light meal before our evening dinner. Sunday dinners were always special and, sometimes, we had company. Usually, Mother fixed fried chicken or a pot roast with three or four vegetables, hot rolls, and a cake or pie. If we had company or it was Easter, Thanksgiving, or Christmas, she might have a ham, an extra vegetable, and both a pie and a cake.

While I liked Mother's cooking, Dad loved it. By the time he was thirty-five, he must have gained at least fifty pounds, based on the pictures I had seen of his younger days. I think that is why his friends called him "Lardy." Even though he grew bigger and rounder as he got older, he was not as soft as he looked, and quite quick when he had to be.

Christmases and Thanksgivings were always happy times. If we did not go to see my cousins in Texola, they came to see us and the whole family was together. Adults and children slept on pallets all over the house, with so many people on the floor it was hard to avoid stepping on someone when I had to go to the bathroom. Every morning, my aunts would complain about the men snoring—especially those who were not their husbands—each wife questioning the other wives how anyone could possibly get any sleep with that racket going on.

In those days, kids in Childress visited a single Santa Claus each year and he only spent one day in town since we knew that he had to get back to the North Pole and make presents for us. He was our special Santa who knew our parents and called each child by name. I usually saw Santa a week or so before Christmas, which was about the same time he visited my cousins in Texola.

On Christmas Day, everyone got up early to see the presents Santa had delivered during the night and exchange gifts with one another. Santa never missed Jean, my cousins, or me, whether we were in Childress or Texola. Almost all of the gifts—except for some of Santa's presents—were handmade or products from the farm. I don't think it mattered because it seemed like everyone really enjoyed whatever they received.

Whenever Mother and my aunts got together, we only ate two formal meals a day—breakfast in the morning and dinner in the evening—but they were spectacular meals. Each wife would cook or bake the specialty for which they were known,

William M. Forsythe

Mother's biscuits and gravy, Aunt Helen's fried chicken and peach cobbler, and Aunt Edna's fresh peas, corn on the cob, and chocolate cake. We usually had a roast, ham, and fried chicken for the special meals, but never turkey.

No one went hungry between meals because we snacked on rolls, cakes, pies, and cookies set out during the day and whatever meats or vegetables were still available from the evening before. Sometimes, my uncles, to my aunts' embarrassment, would undo the top button of their pants for comfort. Belching was common, but never at the table, along with some passing of wind. My cousins and I would look at each other, barely able to keep still from laughing, while the adults just ignored the smell and our snickering.

During the day between meals, the women sat around the kitchen, catching up on family gossip and adding new tales of their own. My dad and uncles, if it was warm enough to sit outside, smoked pipes and cigars—Dad smoked both at the same time in his usual manner—while drinking coffee and talking about the weather and politics. The people in my family shared several truths: All politicians were crooks; Bankers were almost as bad; and the Federal Government was the cause of their problems. During the confabulations, my cousins and I played outside in the barn if we were in Texola or at the railroad yards when my kin was in Childress.

Two weeks before Thanksgiving and Christmas, the creamery operated a turkey processing business in an old tin building across the street from the creamery. Company employees would grab a live turkey from the pen next door to the building, kill and bleed it out, then dunk the carcass in a barrel of boiling water before hanging the scalded body by the feet on a big steel hook, ready for removing the feathers.

An Unsung Hero: Coming of Age in the Dust Bowl

Anyone—adult or kid—could go in and collect a nickel for each turkey they plucked clean. At times, people, mostly adults, filled the building, either picking or waiting for a space to open where they could pick. During the years when Dad was out of work and his poker playing was slow, Mother and Dad worked a few days for extra money. I suspect their experiences were the reason we never ate turkey at home. Between the ages of eight and ten, my friends and I always picked a couple of turkeys on Saturday morning to have enough money to go to the movies in the afternoon.

Plucking turkey feathers was no easy task. The work was dirty, messy, and the building smelled as bad as it looked. Blood, feathers, and hot water from the barrels covered the slippery, concrete floor. There were usually eighty to a hundred carcasses waiting for processing. Most people pulled the body feathers out first since they usually came off without much effort; pulling the smaller wing feathers was more difficult. The pinfeathers—the small feathers growing close to the skin—were the most difficult to remove since they had to be pulled loose one at a time. Some birds had more feathers than other birds so an experienced plucker tried to select a bird that looked like picking would be easy. Prior to being paid, a company inspector checked each plucked bird; if the bird did not suit him, the plucker pulled out more pinfeathers. Adults usually picked eight to ten hours a day, taking twenty to thirty minutes per bird and earning more than a dollar for the day's work.

The Christmas of 1932, times were especially hard. Dad was out of work and we were living on his poker winnings. Jean was three years old and I was eight. The winter was bitterly cold and snow blanketed the streets of Childress—so much snow that special engines with mounted plows had to

William M. Forsythe

clear the rails so the trains could run through the Panhandle. It was impossible for us to drive to Texola or for my aunts and uncles to come to Childress. The snow in my neighborhood was so deep that Dad carried me from the house to the street each morning so I could walk to school in the mashed-down snow and ice ruts of old car tracks. The snow was too high for my friends and I to walk side by side, so we trailed after each other in a long line. Every few houses, a parent carried another kid to the street to join our caravan. It was that kind of winter.

Dad had blocked up our car in the garage because we did not have twelve dollars to license it that year. A couple of weeks before Christmas, Mother asked me to bring some apple crates home so she could make my sister Jean a little table and two chairs using the wood from the crates. In previous years when we could not afford to buy a Christmas tree, Dad drove out in the country and cut a cedar tree for Christmas. That year, we could neither buy one nor go out and cut one because of the snow. Dad cut a big tree limb from one of the trees in our yard, put it in a bucket of dirt to stand straight, and Mother wrapped the trunk in green crepe paper and the limbs in red. She hung the few ornaments we had and Jean and I strung popcorn for decorations.

On Christmas morning, my sister woke up to find a homemade red dress, a little green tea table, chairs, and a little tea set that Mother had scrabbled together. I had a slightly used football that was as good as new and a shirt Mother had made. Our stockings, which we had hung in the kitchen the night before, bulged with apples, oranges, nuts, and Christmas candy. Santa had also left some peppermint canes hanging on the tree. I thought we had the prettiest tree ever and it was my best Christmas ever. While those presents might not seem like much, none of the other kids in the neighborhood got more and I was thrilled to have a football, even though it was second-hand.

There have been many Christmases since that one, most of which I cannot remember details. However, I have never forgotten that year because the winter was so hard and my parents made something special out of love, the little they had, and a tree limb from the front yard.

9 Country Cousins

We made regular trips to Texola after we moved to Childress since most of our Mother's kinfolks lived there. Although only sixty-six miles apart, the trip seemed like a thousand because it was impossible to drive more than twenty or thirty miles an hour on the dirt roads. When it rained, the road over Buck Creek between Childress and Texola flooded and we had to pay a man with a team of mules to pull the car across.

There was hardly a trip we made that we did not have one or more flat tires along the way. Tires went flat frequently. Filling stations were primitive and far apart, so drivers had to change their own flats. When we went to Texola or headed home, Mother tried to have two spare tires with us, "just in case." If we had a spare, changing a flat was easy—Mother jacked up the car, took off the flat tire, put on the spare tire, let down the jack, and we were on our way.

When we got to Texola or home, one of my uncles or Dad would repair the flat tire's inner tube for use as a spare on the next trip. Repairing the inner tube was hard and tedious work. The first task required the removal of the collapsed tube from inside the flat tire—usually by stomping the tire off the rim. Invariably, Dad banged his ankle against the steel edge—a painful experience accompanied by Dad's infrequent use of "Damn it!" and "Hellfire!"

After removing the inner tube, the next step was to find the leak. Dad filled a pail with water and inflated the inner tube with a manual air pump by standing on the pump's flanges while he forced the cylinder inside the pump up and down as quickly as possible. When the inner tube was semi-inflated, he dipped it into the pail of water and looked for telltale bubbles of air to identify the leak. Quickly pulling the tube from the water, he used chalk to mark the leak with a big white X.

Service stations and tire stores sold patch kits that contained several different sizes of precut-rubber patches, "vulcanize" patches, and a small, tin tube of adhesive for a cold patch. Dad did not trust cold patches, so he used the vulcanize patches. He roughed up the surface area around the leak with a steel file, positioned the patch in place, and clamped a small tin box over the patch and tube. He then put little pieces of paper or cloth in the box and set them on fire. The fire, hotter than usual due to the vulcanizing chemical mixture, melted the patch to adhere it to the inner tube and seal the leak. The hardest part was over. All that remained was to put the inner tube back into the tire, the tire on the wheel and, hoping for a good seal, inflate the inner tube a second time. If the seal was not good, he repeated the process; if the seal held, the tire was ready for use as a spare.

While repairing an inner tube was time-consuming, tedious, and often frustrating, filling stations charged a quarter to fix a flat tire, money most people did not have to spare. When I was eleven or twelve, Dad transferred the responsibility of changing flats and repairing inner tubes to me. I did not like the chore any better than he had.

Tire makers quit putting their names on tires because flat tires occurred so often. When a flat occurred, their customers would see the name and say, "I'll never buy that damn tire again." Regardless of make, most cars used the same-sized tire—600x16. Consequently in those days, the tires on a car often came from four different tire makers, especially since most people did not have the money to buy four new tires at a time. A car owner usually bought two new tires for the front; used the best two of the older tires on the rear wheels; and kept the third best tire for a spare.

Most of the times, Mother and I went alone to Texola and took all morning to make the drive. Sometimes I was so anxious to see my cousins that I wanted to get out and run. When the government finally paved the road in the late 1930s, we went in the morning and came home the same day. Until I got to junior high school, I spent weeks in the summers, having a great time with my cousins in the country.

My mother's brothers—Coke, Homer, and Ernest Forsyth—were kindly, though serious men and as different physically as it is possible to be. Coke was tall—well over six foot—and muscular with a deep voice and a politician's gift of gab. Homer was shorter and rounder with weak eyes so he was never without his rimless glasses resting part way down his nose. He was thoughtful, always considering his words before he spoke. Uncle Ernest was almost as tall as Uncle Coke, but as thin as a rail. He was very quiet—rarely starting a conversation, a silent listener lurking on the periphery. I knew him the least because he never talked to me even when we were alone. I never had a Grandpa growing up, but my uncles could not have treated me better; I thought they were great.

Uncle Homer, his wife, Aunt Edna, and my two girl cousins, Lura Fay and Addie Ruth, lived in one house and had a farm they owned and worked with Uncle Ernest, just outside of town. Lura Fay was a little older than me and had her father's brown hair and disposition—always extra nice, but careful to obey her parents' rules even when they were not present. Addie Ruth was my age and took after her black-haired mother—loud and laughing, ready to take any dare without thinking about the danger or the trouble she might find as a result. I enjoyed being with both of them, but Addie Ruth was the most fun. The girls had chores when they were little—feeding chickens, gathering eggs, and helping their mother with cooking and washing. My uncle and aunt sold eggs and cream for cash. Like most farmers, they charged everything they bought from a store until the crops came in.

Uncle Coke, his wife, Aunt Helen, and their kids—Marilyn and Gardis—lived on another farm outside of Texola, but it was too far to go back and forth between the farm and town every day. Marilyn and Gardis, several years younger than me, played with Jean. However, when we went to Texola, the whole family always got together to catch up on the latest news and share work that required more than one family.

Grandma Forsyth, Ernest, and Mother's two younger sisters, Irma and Til, lived in another house about four blocks away from Uncle Homer's house. Texola was much smaller than Childress—about 600 people then—with farms outside of towns and families who came into town on the weekends to shop.

Grandma's house had a parlor used only when company visited. The family lived mostly in the big kitchen and three bedrooms. In the kitchen was a big, iron, wood-burning cook stove, two big enameled metal cabinets, and a large rectangular wooden table with chairs around one side and the two ends of the table, with a bench for the other side.

I do not remember much about Grandma except that she had long, grey hair that went down to her waist. She brushed her hair every morning and put it up in a bun. When we visited, Mother sometimes brushed her hair while they talked.

None of the women in the family smoked, but Grandma dipped snuff that she bought in little Garrett Sweet Snuff glasses. When sitting in her rocking chair on the front porch, she would take a small green twig, chew on it to splinter the end, and use it as her "snuff brush." She stuck the brush into the can of snuff, put it into her mouth for the "dip," and discreetly spit from time to time into a small can she kept for that purpose. When she emptied a jar, she rubbed the label off, washed it, and the family used it for a small drinking glass.

When we stayed at Uncle Homer's house, I slept in a trundle bed with Lura and Addie Ruth. During the day, Aunt Edna shoved the smaller bed under the bigger bed until night. Uncle Homer had a large hay barn where we played. He had taken an old wagon wheel axle, removed one of the wheels, and buried the axle in the ground to make a perfect merry-go-round.

There were only plowed fields in front of their house, but the cotton gin where my uncles worked was next door. We often played on the giant cotton bales until the bales went to market. The town had no sidewalks or paved streets so we couldn't skate or ride scooters. Our play was limited to the barn, merry-go-round, cotton bales, and whatever adventures we could find in the country around us.

All of the family went to the town's Church of Christ except Uncle Coke and his family. When he married Aunt Helen, I think he became a Presbyterian. The day before church, Aunt Edna cooked the unleavened bread and Uncle Homer furnished the grape juice for the Lord's Supper every Sunday.

My cousins living in the country had no electricity, no gas, no running water, no icebox, and no inside toilet. When they bathed, it was in a No. 3 washtub. Aunt Edna heated water in a teakettle on the wood-burning stove, poured it into the tub, and mixed in water from the well to get the temperature right. Stoves were essential—used for cooking, warming the house in the winter, and heating metal irons to press clothes, in addition to fixing the bath water.

My uncles Homer and Ernest worked at the gin when it was open and farmed when they were not at the gin. Every morning, they hitched a team to a wagon and went about two and one-half miles north of town to their farm. They kept their plows and farm tools in a shed at the farm. There were two small, unpainted, wooden houses on piers about a foot off the ground. Each house had an eight-foot, plank porch that extended across its front for sleeping. The families moved to the farm in the summers. Everyone slept on the porches or on pallets in the yard, except Grandma who slept inside, no matter how hot it might be.

My family slept outside in Childress too when it became unbearably hot. The most magnificent sights I have ever seen were the night skies in those days. I would stretch out on my back and look up at the stars—sparkling from horizon to horizon. Sometimes, I counted shooting stars—seeing four or five at a time plummet across the blackness—until I fell asleep. My uncles taught me most of the constellations by the time I was ten, although I sometimes had difficulty remembering every star in their composition.

The stars in the country were even brighter than in Childress. The sky looked like a carpet of small flickering lights with an occasional sparkle here and there more radiant than elsewhere. I could hear coyotes howl at the moon at night in Texola. One would start, then another. Before too long, four or five were howling from all directions around us. The aroused dogs ran around excitedly barking until the racket awoke Uncle Homer or Uncle Ernest. One would yell at them, "Be quiet and lay down!" and the dogs did. Uncle Homer trained his dogs well.

A small barn sat between the farmhouses, along with fenced lots for their five cows, two mules, and three horses. A big pigpen with a small, low shed for the hogs to escape the sun squatted next to the barn. It really was not a shed, just a slanted roof on four posts about four feet high. A chicken yard with two or three coops and about sixty chickens was on the other side of the pigsty beside a small—about ten-feet by twenty-feet—vegetable garden where my aunts grew radishes, onions, corn, beans, and watermelons.

The root cellar between the houses had a wooden door that latched from the inside or the outside. The door was too heavy for me to open by myself because, as Uncle Homer explained, they did not want it flying away in a tornado. The cellar was really a hand-dug hole in the ground about ten feet long, eight-feet wide, and seven feet deep with a roof of wooden boards with dirt mounded over the boards. A piece of stovepipe—without a stove—pierced the roof on one end to circulate air inside the cellar. Wooden shelves filled with canned vegetables and fruits covered the walls from floor to wooden ceiling. The end with the cellar door had steps—loose boards hammered into the ground so they would not move or get too slippery when it rained—leading up to the outside. Wooden benches lined each side of the cellar for a place to sit when you were stuck there during a tornado. An oil lamp and a small bottle of kerosene rested on the floor, ready if you needed light.

The root cellar also served as a tornado shelter when needed. That part of Texas and Oklahoma gets violent thunderstorms and ruinous tornadoes during the spring and summer. Cold winds from the north sweep unobstructed to clash with the hot, moisture-laden winds from the south and set off violent electric storms and an occasional twister. I loved watching the lightening dance and streak across the sky, sometimes lighting up the dark clouds with each flash, followed by big booms of thunder that shook the ground. The rain in Texola never fell in gentle showers, but in great globules that splattered and drenched the ground. Sometimes, hail pelted—stones as big as golf balls that rebounded, careening into other stones. Watching a hailstorm was like seeing a giant frying pan of popcorn—the popped corn rebounding and bouncing helter skelter every which way. My uncles, of course, hated hail because it ruined crops growing in the field, but the power and beauty of a rolling thunderstorm continues to awe me and makes me realize how puny I am and how powerful God must be.

All of my cousins' water came from wells. The one at the farm was topped with a wooden A-frame and pulley. Rather than use smaller buckets, my uncles drew water with a thirty-inch length of round galvanized pipe, pinched on one end to prevent the water from leaking out and the other end fastened to a knotted rope that ran through the pulley. Uncle Homer tied the free end of the rope to one of the A-frame posts so the pipe would not accidentally fall into the well. Drinking water came partly from barrels of rainwater collected by rain gutters on each house and partly from the well. No one in the country had running water or sewers.

About twenty yards between the houses, my Texola kin had an outdoor toilet with two holes in the seat. Their "two-holer" had toilet paper and an old Sears catalogue so you could have company or something to read when you went to the toilet. Uncle Homer or Uncle Ernest poured lime down the holes from time to time to make the smell tolerable. The lime worked most of the time, except on the hottest days. For years, there was a medium-sized yellow-jacket nest fastened high in the front right corner with a few wasps always flying around. When I was doing my business, I kept an eye on the nest just in case, but I never got stung. Eventually, my girl cousins talked my uncle into burning the nest out with a rolled up piece of newspaper lit on one end.

People living in the country did not have electricity until the formation of the Rural Electric Administration (REA) formed in 1935. Any light that we had came from the stove or coal oil and kerosene lamps that everybody had. Some people, but not my uncles, did have wind chargers—what some called "electric plants," but not my uncles. Like a windmill that drew water, the wind powered a generator attached to a battery that powered a radio or a single light bulb. It does not sound like much, but in those days, it was a miracle for farm families without electricity to listen to a radio in those days.

People without a good well had to catch rainwater in gutters and pipe it to a cistern. Either way, any water had to be drawn for use one bucket at a time for use. A second bucket for drinking water sat on the porch or by the stove and everyone used the same dipper when they were thirsty. Drinking out of the same ladle was so common that some comics would tease a homely girl or boy by saying they were "so ugly that she/he had to slip up on the dipper to get a drink." I thought the saying was funny, but knowing it was hurtful, I never said it to anyone.

Uncle Homer milked the five cows both mornings and nights after working the fields all day. After milking, he emptied the pails of fresh, warm milk into a large separator to separate the cream from the milk, poured the cream into ten-gallon milk cans, and added the leftover milk to the hog slop.

An Unsung Hero: Coming of Age in the Dust Bowl

Uncle Homer took the cans of cream to town each day, put the load on the train, and shipped it to a creamery.

Everyone worked in the fields—in addition to their other chores—every day except Sunday. My cousins fed the horses and mules and helped with the milking. Farming then was so labor-intensive that everyone in the family worked to survive. A few weeks after school started in September, classes let out to pick cotton. Even the young kids helped get the family cotton into the gins. When I visited, I worked with them or we did not get to be together.

When I was in Texola, either one of my cousins or Grandma cooked breakfast every morning. Grandma had the keenest silverware with wooden handles and very thin, flexible blades. You could almost bend them in a ninety-degree angle, which was great to get the last dollops of pancake syrup off of a plate.

People made coffee by adding the ground coffee beans to a large pot filled with water and heating the pot to boiling on a hot stove or campfire. When the coffee was ready and poured into a cup, it was still boiling and too hot to drink. Consequently, most people spilled a little coffee into a saucer, blew on the liquid to cool it, and slurped it from the saucer until the coffee in the cup cooled enough to drink. The process was noisy, but so what? It looked like their coffee tasted good. Drinking coffee that way was so common that people began saying that nothing was ready until it was "saucered and blowed."

At least a dozen or more fried eggs were served on a plate in the center of the table for breakfast. Crispy, fried bacon strips and ham slices piled up on a platter, bowls of peppered, white flour gravy, hot biscuits that had been made earlier that morning, a big bowl of butter, and jars of sorghum syrup was the usual fare. I loved to eat breakfast at Grandma's or Uncle Homer's house. The girls collected any leftovers in a bucket and fed it to the hogs. Sometimes, I think those pigs ate better than we did at Childress!

My uncles usually slaughtered a couple of hogs in late fall. Uncle Coke and his family would come over early in the morning. One of my uncles shot the hog in the head with a .22 rifle and another jumped in the pen to cut its throat so it bled out. At my first slaughtering, I thought it cruel and ran crying to my mother in the farmhouse. My cousins, not knowing that I had never seen anything killed, didn't know what to say. Mother hugged me as we sat on the steps of the front porch with Lura Fay and Addie Ruth sitting beside me.

"God put animals on earth for Man's benefit. In Genesis, God told Adam that humans were to be masters of every living creature—the birds in the sky, the fish in the sea, and every animal that lives on the land," Mother explained. "God also told us to drain the blood from the animals we slaughter, that it is a sin to eat meat with the blood still in it."

She explained to me that the ham and bacon we ate each day came from pigs and it wasn't cruel to kill animals for food, but a necessary part of life. Killing the hog was no different from killing a chicken by wringing its neck so we could eat chicken. All meat came from animals that were once alive.

Having seen me run away crying and thinking I might be hurt, Uncle Homer came back to the house looking for me.

"Doodle, we kill the hog by shooting him in the brain so he dies instantly and never feels his throat being cut. We don't kill animals in fun; only because we need the meat ourselves," Uncle Homer explained.

"We take care of our animals as best we can—being sure they are fed, have plenty of water, and kept safe during storms or the winter. But animals are animals, not humans, and we are farmers who raise food for other people or cotton for their clothes. It is how we live, just like your Dad works on the railroad."

"Come on back with me. The worst part is over," he said, taking me by my hand. "You can see where ham and bacon comes from and how we make it. And you can tell your friends in town so they will know where their food actually comes from even though their mothers might buy it in a store."

When we got back to the hog pen, I saw that my uncles had lifted the hog into a barrel of simmering water—bubbles of steam burst above the surface into wispy vapor trails in the cool fall morning. After a while, the men tied a rope around the back feet and, using a pulley hung from a tree, lifted the scalded body to hang head down about a foot off the ground. Uncle Homer and Uncle Ernest scraped the body with sharp butcher knives to get all the dirt, hair, and top skin off.

They cut the head off first and then removed all of the insides. I learned later that some people use the head to make headcheese—a kind of meat jelly—but my family never did. They burned the head with the guts after they were finished. When the butchering was over, they had hams, pork chops, ribs, and bacon. Mother, my aunts, and cousins began to make sausage from the smaller pieces, grinding up those pieces too tiny to serve alone and adding different kinds of spices to the mixture. They also salted the meat for hanging in the smokehouse.

The smokehouse was about eight feet square with one door. A long, covered trench carried the heavy smoke from an outside burning fire into the smokehouse. After the meat cured, the hams, bacon, and sides of chops were stored in the smokehouse until needed. I really liked the ham my uncles made; it was a little saltier than you find today, but it tasted exquisite. Whenever we returned from Texola, we always brought back some hams and bacon.

When I was seven, Aunt Til married another Texola man. Uncle Boy became one of my favorite uncles. His dad was the city marshal. To me, his dad looked just like an old-time sheriff ought to look with a big western hat, a star on his chest, a pistol in a holster on his hip, and white hair. Uncle Boy and Aunt Til were married just after Oklahoma passed a state sales tax and established ports of entry where every truck and trailer entering the state had to stop, register, and pay a tax. Texola was the Port of Entry into Oklahoma for trucks and cars coming east on Highway 66.

Uncle Boy owned service stations on three of the four corners at the Port of Entry. Since every truck and trailer had to stop at one of his stations anyway, he opened a cold drink stand next to them. When I was older and went to Texola, I stayed with him and Aunt Til so I could run their stand part-time. Lura Fay and Addie Ruth had chores and other things they did during the day so I worked in the stand for something to do. That was fine with me.

Uncle Boy sold candy, soda pop, and chewing gum, along with mints, and miscellaneous items from the stand. Sales tax was calculated and paid in mills—a fraction of a penny. The five-mill coin was brass, and the one-mill coins were aluminum. I do not remember how many mills I had to collect for each dollar, but everything in the store sold for a nickel. I never sold more than a quarter's worth at any one time. During the summer of 1936, I spent almost the whole summer in Texola—working in the stand, hunting, and riding horses.

Sometimes, Jean and I stayed with Uncle Coke's family, but, with my cousins being so young, I had nothing to do. Knowing I was bored, Uncle Coke would invite me to help him deliver his rural mail route. He had a Model A Ford with the starter on the steering wheel, which I thought was pretty neat. The two of us got up early, went to the Texola post office where he sorted mail, and off we went. It usually took about four hours to deliver the route. When we finished, we drove back to the post office to leave the outgoing mail we had collected on the route, and then returned to the farm where Uncle Coke still had work to do.

Uncle Coke had an old horse with a stiff leg named Frank. Whenever I rode him, Uncle Cole warned me not to run him because he was likely to stumble and throw me. Not being able to trot didn't bother me since riding was always better than walking. Frank and I walked to hunt rabbits and sometimes over to Uncle Homer's farm to see Lura Fay and Addie Ruth. It was about three miles as the crow flies and about an hour's ride. I would ride over in Texas and come back in Oklahoma. When you are alone on horseback, you have time to do lots of thinking and daydreaming. I shot Indians under every bush, pretended to drive cattle, and sang to pass the time.

One winter when we were in Texola, Addie Ruth and I decided to ride old Frank bareback. We rode off into a north wind for about an hour. I rode behind Addie Ruth with my arms around her waist to keep her steady and holding the reins. When we started home, Old Frank, knowing he was going home to a warm stall, got in a hurry. The more I pulled the reins and yelled, "whoa," the faster he ran. When we saw the fence in front of the house, I just knew Frank was going to try to jump it. He did not. He stopped at the last instant. Addie Ruth and I flew over his head, over the fence, and hit the ground. I do not believe I have ever felt a blow as hard. It knocked the wind out of me, but Addie Ruth was unscathed. She was mad at me for bouncing her on the horse's neck during the run, but started laughing as I bent over gasping, trying to get my breath. I don't remember riding horses with her again—not because she was mad, but we never had another opportunity.

When I stayed with Uncle Coke after the cotton was planted, I usually "chopped cotton" with Aunt Helen. Chopping cotton is not actually chopping the cotton plants, but cutting the weeds with a sharp hoe around each of the growing plants. Aunt Helen and I walked down adjacent furrows, chopping weeds on the rows of cotton on each side, so that we were able to weed two rows at a time. We chopped to the end of one furrow, moved over, and chopped two more rows coming back. By the time we got back to the water jug where we started, we had chopped out four rows. Unfortunately, a field of cotton usually had a lot of rows.

One year, Uncle Coke raised broomcorn. Broomcorn is actually a kind of sorghum that grows about six feet high and has a top that looks like the stems of a broom—the reason for its name. I thought it looked like a corn stalk with an upside down broom growing right out the top of the stalk. A field of broomcorn looks like a field of brooms sticking up in the air— a broom on each stalk. I helped harvest it the summer I was about thirteen. Aunt Helen drove the wagon while Uncle Coke and I walked on opposite sides. As we walked along on our side, each of us cut the brooms off the plants with a sharp knife and tossed them into the wagon. Carrying bundles of stalks was the worst part of the work because the chaff drifted down your back and neck and made your skin itch like crazy. When we finished each day, we went down to the windmill where Uncle Coke had built a shower and washed off. That felt good.

To me back in those days, a trip to Texola was like a trip to the Garden of Eden. Grandma was a great cook, as were Aunt Edna, Aunt Helen, and Aunt Til. We always had the best meals. I loved Lura and Addie Ruth like they were my own sisters. We rode horses, drove the wagons, played in barns and on cotton bales, swam in the stock tank, and roamed all over the countryside.

When we were older, Addie Ruth and I hunted rabbits in the pastures. If she did not want to go, I rode out on one of the horses and hunted alone. It was a different life for me, and I made the most of it.

Nearly every summer, I spent a couple of weeks at Turkey, Texas visiting Mother's first cousins who lived in the country and at least a dozen second cousins who lived in town. Grandma Forsyth had a lot of family in Turkey, a small town about fifty miles west of Childress. Originally because of the number of wild turkey roosts, the settlement was called Turkey Creek, but was shortened to Turkey as time went by. The town had been founded about the same time as Texola. Bob Wills—the man some people called the "King of Western Swing" —was a barber in Turkey in the 1920s. He had already moved on when I started visiting.

One of Grandma's brothers, Uncle Erb, farmed outside the town. I saw him every summer when I went to Turkey. Mary, Grandma's sister, was married to Fred Lacy who owned the only hotel in town. Another sister was married to Albert, Fred's brother, the owner of the hardware store. Two other sisters were married to farmers, one man named Bunk and the other Perry Wilson. Mother's cousins owned just about every business in town.

When I visited in the summer summer, I rode the train alone from Childress to Turkey and spent a couple of weeks living between my great-uncles' homes. I always had a great time with lots of "cousins", though they were actually second cousins since the relatives were great-uncles and great-aunts, being Grandma's sisters and their husbands.

Kenner, one of my second cousins and the son of Uncle Perry and Aunt Lou, was just a few years older than I. Kenner had a beautiful black horse named Tar Baby that he taught to do tricks like counting numbers or rearing up when he raised his arm. The two of us would go to a lake on their property and swim with the horse. We stripped off our clothes, took the saddle and bridle off Tar Baby, and jumped in the lake. Sometimes I rode her while she swam or held onto her tail and let her pull me through the water. That was great fun for a city boy.

Uncle Perry thought he was a funny man. His favorite joke was to hook two wires to an old wind-up phone on the wall, put a silver dollar in a wash pan of water, and put one of the wires in the pan. Then he would hand you the other wire to hold while he turned the crank. Uncle Perry would tell the kids that whoever could take the silver dollar out of the water while he cranked could have it. Turning the crank produced a shock to anyone holding the wire with his hand in the water—the faster he cranked, the more intense the shock. I never got the dollar, but I sure tried.

Mother's oldest brother, Uncle Luther, and his family also lived on a farm near Turkey and I stayed with them sometimes. Uncle Luther had three children—one boy named Melvin a couple years older than me, a daughter about my age,

An Unsung Hero: Coming of Age in the Dust Bowl

and a son about seven years younger. Melvin worked in the fields every day but Sunday. I usually chopped cotton right beside him so we could visit.

Melvin was fun to be around when we finished work. He would either let me ride calves or take me coon hunting at night. The two of us would take his dog and be out until two or three in the morning hunting. It was fun, but required a lot of walking and running when the dog got a scent. Farming was hard then and Uncle Luther never had much time to spend with me, but I enjoyed visiting his family.

All the families in town went to the Church of Christ on Sundays. Their church was a big, white, frame building with wide, tall windows—usually opened—down each side of the buildings. Sometimes, the kids sat outside under a window to listen to the preacher and sing with the congregation when it was time for a song. During Communion, the adults in the building passed the bread and wine out the window to us. It was a one-cup church so everyone sipped from the same cup for the Lord's Supper. I liked going to church that way.

10 Roosevelt is Elected

After winning the 1932 Presidential election by a landslide, Franklin D. Roosevelt began office and went right to work. He passed the National Recovery Act through Congress, but the Supreme Court declared it unconstitutional by a vote of four members to three members. The President appointed two more judges, packing the Court in his favor, and the new Court declared the same bill Constitutional by a vote of five to four. The Act introduced the eight-hour working day. Roosevelt created the Civil Conservation Corps and the National Youth Administration to put men and boys to work building bridges, parks, and roads. Things began to look a little better and people were hopeful that the worst was over.

Because depositors were withdrawing their money from banks and creating a financial panic, the President closed all the banks. When he re-opened the banks, he promised that the government would protect bank depositors up to $100,000. His actions stopped the runs on banks. He also made it illegal for citizens to own gold and exchanged the gold metal in their possession for Federal Reserve Notes. This move took the country's monetary system off the gold standard. As a consequence, many people believed he saved the country's financial system. Others complained that his actions made United States currency worthless. I do not know who was right, but I liked him for doing something.

At that time, our nearly new 1929 Graham Paige car had been up on blocks in the garage for almost a year. Unable to find other work, Dad took the car out of storage and started a taxi service. He used the pay phone in the cafe next to the YMCA for customers to call him. He serviced the car, printed business cards advertising a 10-cent taxi service, and went to work. Most of the railroaders on the visiting trains rode taxis when they wanted to go downtown to eat or spend the night. Dad knew the men from playing poker and got all of their business while continuing to play in their nightly game. The effect of providing a taxi to the same men in his poker game had some funny consequences. When he won a big pot from a particular player, the other men would tease the losing player that Dad sent a taxi to get him because his poker playing was so bad.

Prior to the big lay-offs, the railroad company sponsored a ball team with Dad as the manager and coach. Watching baseball in the early thirties, especially on Sunday afternoons, was popular because it was free. Dad was popular as the team's manager, which helped his taxi business. About six months after starting the taxi business, he hired a second driver, purchased a newer, second car, and moved his office from the cafe to a rented space uptown. Later that year, Dad acquired one of the other cab companies in town so he had a three-car company. About the same time, he bought a pool hall, a domino parlor, and combined the offices of the three companies.

We caught up on the back rent and Dad loaned or gave money to our relatives that needed help. We were not rich by any means, but we had the cars and the other businesses. A year later, the railroad called Dad back to work and allowed him to keep his side businesses. He still played poker in the YMCA games, but not as often and not as cutthroat. Neither he nor Mother complained when the grocery bill went to $20 a month.

With the repeal of Prohibition in 1933, cities and counties of Texas determined by vote whether to allow the sale of liquor in their communities, a choice called the "local option." Like many small towns with active church memberships, Childress always "drank wet, but voted dry." To get around the law, retired doctors developed a thriving business writing prescriptions for liquor. The Childress law allowed a person to buy a pint of whiskey each day for health reasons. The prescribing doctor got twenty-five cents for writing the prescription from the pharmacist and the drug store got a good, repeat customer. I did not know any of the doctors who were writing prescriptions since they did not live in Childress. I assumed they were retired from practices in nearby towns, but never knew for sure. The practice of writing phony prescriptions has always been unethical, if not illegal, and eventually, the Sheriff enforced the law when citizens complained about the flagrant violations.

One of Dad's cab stations was next door to a drug store heavily involved in the liquor business; we made lots of money delivering those prescription pints of liquor for the pharmacist to "sick" folks. My dad never drank any kind of alcohol and everyone who knew him knew he did not drink. A couple years later, when new owners bought an old, vacant building in the same block of Dad's office, they found a pile of empty whiskey bottles with prescriptions pasted on them, all in the name of my dad, Virgil Lewis, or the town's only Baptist preacher, Reverend Hankins.

As I thought about it, I realized that a customer with a prescription could only buy one pint of whiskey each day. If he wanted more than a pint, he had to get a second prescription in the name of another person who might by chance be purchasing whiskey for himself on the same day.

The safest way to ensure that he got his extra liquor was to use the name of someone he knew who was not a drinker and would not be buying a pint for his own use the same day.

I started my own businesses, too. After persuading the railroad shop boss to give me the railroad's empty fifty-five gallon barrels in return for disposing of them, I sold them around town as trash barrels. For fifty cents, I would wash out the barrel and roll it down the streets to my customer's house. After I got through the first set of old barrels, there was not much of a business left since the railroad only used one barrel each week.

The following year, I began delivering the *Wichita Falls Post* each week. I met the Sunday passenger train from Wichita Falls at 4:30 AM and deliver papers all over town. I bought a new bike on credit and paid a dollar a week on the debt from the earnings of my paper route. After school each day, I washed dishes for a cafe near our house and earned a dime for a couple hours of work. I washed dishes for a half year, but didn't like the work or my lack of free time.

Having my own money was great, but I wanted a job that paid the most for the least amount of work, or with a schedule so that I worked when my friends were not available. I kept my paper route for a couple of years, but mostly relied on odd jobs and scavenging for other income.

When I was thirteen, I offered to work for free at Meacham's grocery store if the owner would hire me once I learned the ropes. At the end of the first Saturday, he tried to pay me a quarter for my work, but I turned him down, explaining that was not our deal.

"If you thought I was a good worker, you promised to give me a job every Saturday," I said. He laughed, put the quarter back in his pocket, and said, "You're hired. Be here by seven next Saturday."

For the next six months, I worked every Saturday for twenty-five cents a day. One Saturday, he asked me if I would like to deliver groceries in the store's pickup after school each day for two hours and all day Saturdays for $2.25 per week. I was in the big money! And I got to drive the pick-up around town!

To make a little extra money, I bought boxes of candy from the Royal Crown Bottling Company—twenty-four bars for eighty cents—and peddled candy bars around downtown for a nickel a bar, making forty cents in profit per box. Sometimes I went to Dad's domino parlor and sold the whole box within an hour. Some bars of candy had a white spot inside the wrapper that entitled the buyer to a second bar free. I gave the buyer a free bar in exchange for the wrapper and the bottling company gave me a nickel for it. The chance to win a free bar gave the buyer a little something extra for his money, but didn't cost me anything. That was a good business strategy.

In the 30s, games of chance were legal. Pinball machines and one-armed bandit slot machines paid off in coins right out of the machine. Punchboards were plentiful and there were different kinds. There was one where the punched spot decided the size of the candy bar you received for your nickel and another that entitled the puncher to a little gift—the type of gift depending upon the sponsor of the punchboard.

An Unsung Hero: Coming of Age in the Dust Bowl

My dad was lucky on punchboards, sometimes winning the grand prize before all of the spots on the board sold. Usually, after the grand prize was gone, the board was worthless. Merchants started adding other, less expensive prizes to the board to keep interest up and make gamblers think the purchase was worth the risk even if the big prize had been won. Later in the decade, the Texas Legislature outlawed games of chance—including punchboards and pinball machines.

With Dad's businesses going well, the worst days of the Depression were over for us. We bought a new cook stove, a gas refrigerator that replaced our icebox, a new Atwater-Kent radio, and moved into a three-bedroom house. Listening to a radio program required an antenna on the top of the house that connected to the radio with a second wire from the radio that was stuck into the ground. Whenever there was static on the radio, Dad sent me outside to pour water on the ground around the wire. Sometimes it helped and sometimes not. As more families got radios, kids did not spend as much time outside playing. Programs like *Robert Armstrong*, *Dick Tracy*, *Little Orphan Annie*, and *Green Hornet* came on right after school and were popular with everyone. Fortunately, most programs were only fifteen minutes long, so we still had time to play when they were over.

A couple of times a year, President Roosevelt had a special program to talk about the problems of the country. Mother and Dad always sat and listened, but most kids were not interested in his speeches. Sometimes, Dad made a comment about the President, Congress, or what he thought the government was doing wrong or should be doing; but Mother, usually sewing, rarely responded. Mostly, they listened to radio stations in Dallas and Ft Worth that carried no news, but plenty of music. The folks especially liked to listen to Ft Worth's WBAP—a station that broadcast the Light Crust Doughboys with Bob Wills who, before becoming popular, had lived in Turkey, the home of Grandma Forsyth.

A "Helpy-Selfy" laundry with Maytag three-tub washing machines opened within a couple of blocks of our house about 1936. Few people could afford to buy a washing machine, so it was a godsend for housewives and mothers. Mother went to the laundry once a week instead of washing with a rubbing board and a No.3 washtub. She filled several wicker baskets with dirty clothes, towels, and sheets, loaded them on my old red wagon from childhood, and walked to the laundry pulling the wagon behind her. Separate laundry stalls—each with a Maytag and its three tubs configured in a square—filled the building. Mom washed the laundry in scalding hot water in the washing machine, then took each piece out, one by one with a wooden stick and ran it through a set of rollers to squeeze the hot water out. She then plunged the still hot piece into a tub of cold "bluing" water to set off the white colors. She continued sequentially into the two other tubs to rinse the soap from the washed clothes. The final step was to run each piece through a second roller system to wring as much water as possible out of the fabric before folding and stacking it into the wicker baskets for the trip home. The laundry cost fifteen cents per load, but one load was enough for most people in those days. In fact, the price was considered such a bargain that even widows and women who took in laundry and ironing for a fee used the Helpy-Selfy.

When Mother got home, she hung the damp clothes on lines in the backyard to dry in the sun. Companies have tried to replicate the air-dried, fresh fragrance of clothes since that time with chemicals, but their efforts never smell quite right. For Mother, the washing machine was probably the greatest invention of the 1930s, taking the drudgery and hard work out of what had been a weekly, all day chore.

Mom and Dad never recovered from those harsh days of worrying about where every penny went and whether or not Dad could find work. They were never able to spend money freely or for what they called "frivolous things." Mother and Dad worried and worked hard to get through the bad times. I often wonder if I could have done it in their place.

I will never forget how people helped one another, despite the poverty and the uncertainty of the future. We never locked our doors or worried about theft or robbery. People gave what they could to those in need. Grocery stores and service stations sold on credit and trusted their customers and neighbors to pay when and what they were able. Some landlords let people live in their houses rent-free or delayed rent until times were better. I am not sure that our society today would be as generous.

William M. Forsythe

11 The Winds Come

People thought the hard times of the Depression could not get worse, then in 1934 the drought came and with it…the winds. Uncle Homer's well at the farm went dry so he hauled water from anyplace he could find it—mostly from another farm by the river three miles away where the well hadn't gone dry. My uncles and their neighbors had to haul water in fifty-gallon barrels on horse-drawn sleds. Uncle Homer usually filled two barrels covered with white denim to keep the dust out of the water and tied with a rope to the sled to keep them from tipping over. Two horses were needed to pull the sled. In their common hardship, everybody shared what he or she had, even, I believe, their last piece of bread if it had been needed.

The drought had begun earlier in the decade, drying out the land and killing most of the crops in Texas, Oklahoma, Kansas, and Arkansas. When farmers could not pay back the money borrowed to make a crop, the banks foreclosed on their land. As the land dried, the winds began to blow, often for days at a time without stopping, rolling up the topsoil and carrying it for hundreds of miles. Some days, the dust was so thick you could not see the sun. People wrapped bandanas over their faces just to breathe.

The dust and sand storms were terrible and almost indescribable. A sandstorm appeared in the distance hours before it arrived—the dark red sky rolling and boiling until the sand cloud blanketed everything, blocking out the sun and lasting for days. Lura and Addie Ruth said they could not see the blackboard from the back of their schoolroom with all of the dust in the air, even though the teachers shut the windows and doors as tightly as possible and layered wet cloths in the sills.

At my uncles' homes, the high pitched, shrill sound of a whistle accompanied the wind blowing through cracks around the doors and windows. The linoleum that had been glued to the floors lifted and the wallpaper seemed to breathe in and out. Nothing kept the sand out. Even when there seemed to be no visible openings, the sand drifted in and covered every surface with a thin layer of dust. Sometimes, so much sand would blow in their houses that my uncles had to use grain shovels to clean out the deposits of dirt. And the winds blew again the next day.

The topsoil of thousands of farms melted away in the continuous battering of the wind, leaving behind bare hardpan. Nothing withstood the storms—crops, animals, buildings or humans. When the wind stopped, sand drifts two and three feet high settled in black and brown piles against the houses, barns, and fence posts. Uncle Homer lost the topsoil on his fields, leaving nothing but sandblow. Sand covered the fences, obscuring any possibility of telling where one field ended and another began, what was one man's property and where his neighbor's began. Even small trees and bushes disappeared in the drifted sand. And the wind kept blowing!

The Federal government tried to help and encouraged farmers to build "Shelter Belts" in an effort to stop the erosion of the topsoil. When driving through that part of Texas and Oklahoma today, you can still see lines of closely planted trees, three and four deep, beside roads and between fields.

They are the remnants of the old Shelter Belts. I recognize them on sight, even though it was more than sixty years ago.

When the drought came, the crops withered away in the field, leaving nothing to harvest or enough vegetation for animals to forage. For all intents and purpose, the farms disappeared. My uncles and their family's only income came from the sale of eggs from the chickens and cream from the cows. They had nothing else to sell but livestock that no one wanted. Most farmers had more livestock than they could feed. The lowest point came one night while my cousins were at church. Someone, a neighbor or a tramp passing through, stole all of their chickens and any potential egg money. My uncle asked my dad soon after, "What do you do when you have nowhere to go, but you can't stay here?" Dad did not answer, just stood there shaking his head and looked out over the wasteland that had been a fertile green landscape less than five years before.

Dad had grown up with two sisters, but loved the Forsyth men as if they were his brothers. When he and Mother married, they had accepted him as one of their own. Despite their church's teachings, they overlooked his gambling and occasional bootlegging without question or condemnation. During his own financial hardship, they had helped him whenever they had extra money. My dad knew knew the door was always open for him and his family.

"Homer, I know things are tough now and they may not get better for farmers for a long time," Dad said. "I don't have any answers, but I want you to know that things are going well for Faye and me. The cab company is doing better than I expected. A friend of mine at the railroad told me that it looks like I'll be going back to work soon. We have some extra money saved. It is there if you or the other boys need it."

Uncle Homer did not speak. What could he say? A few minutes later, both men turned and walked toward the house. My dad, his ever-present pipe with cigar puffing smoke over both men's heads, patted Homer on his back. We sat down for supper and Uncle Homer said Grace over the food. That day was the same as most of our visits except the fields were brown and bare—almost the same color as the Childress train yard stained by years of discarded oil and grease.

Farming for my uncles or any farmer in the Panhandle did not get better. Cows were so cheap that the price of a bred milk cow or a cow with a calf was only $15-$20, but there were no buyers at any price. Hoping the market would rise if there were less supply, the Federal Government bought thousands of cows and shipped them to central locations where they were shot and buried. When I was about twelve, I watched a slaughter outside of Texola with my uncles. Riflemen sitting on the fences around a corral shot hundreds of animals. When the bodies of the dead cattle were removed for burial, a new herd was led into the enclosure, and the shooting continued. It went all day long. The ground turned to mud from the blood. The air was thick with gorged flies and the sweet odor of death.

Despite the need for food, few cows were sent to a Government packing plant to be canned and distributed to the needy. Hungry people, unemployed for months, begged the Government men to give them a cow for slaughter or to let them butcher a carcass for food, but the men ignored their pleas and buried the bodies in a giant pit scraped by large bulldozers. The bulldozers mounded the grave with more dirt to ensure people did not try to open the grave to salvage meat. Some people never forgave their neighbors—the men doing the shooting—for the deed. However, the riflemen had families themselves and needed the job; they had nothing to do with the decision to bury the cows.

Farm products were hardly worth taking to market. Some farmers burned their wheat for fuel since wheat was cheaper than coal. The government finally started paying farmers to plow up cotton, corn, and wheat in an effort to raise prices.

When the dust storms began to abate, the boils appeared. We called them "risens." Boils and carbuncles—painful, pus-filled lumps—erupted on people's faces, necks, and armpits, making them miserable. In the worst cases, fever and chills accompanied the boils. Some had only one or two while others had a dozen or more. One boy down the street had forty at one time.

Boils affected every one, rich and poor, men and women, young and old. They usually started with a single red bump, tender to the touch that grew quickly until it burst in a flood of yellow pus with the infection causing even more boils to arise within days. Not knowing better, mothers put poultices of bacon on the sore to draw the infection to the surface. When a small white head appeared, a needle was heated over an open flame to kill any germs and plunged it into the head of the boil, squeezing the lump beneath the skin as tightly as possible to force all of the pus to the surface. The treatment hurt tremendously and I always screamed and cried when Mother opened one of mine.

Surprisingly, Dad never had a boil, but some men got four or five in the same spot on the back of their necks. These were

An Unsung Hero: Coming of Age in the Dust Bowl

usually opened by a doctor, leaving a silver dollar-sized scar that all could see. Walking down the street, I would see four or five men with a scar or a carbuncle that would become a scar above their shirt collars. No one at the time knew their cause—some thought drinking too much milk was the culprit; others believe eating salt pork or not bathing enough was the reason.

The preachers said it was a plague like the one God had visited upon the Egyptians in the Old Testament. They said God caused the misery of the dust and boils because men were evil with their drinking, lying, and running around with married women. Our salvation and freedom from the boils went hand in hand—relief only possible by confessing our sins and repenting. Men and women, and a few boys, filled the aisles of our little church whenever the preacher called for sinners to come forth and proclaim their sinfulness publicly. Perhaps the preachers were right—the affliction disappeared as mysteriously as it arrived.

When the dust and sand storms finally ended, Texola lost a lot of its glamour for me. Uncle Homer borrowed money from Dad, quit farming, and moved to Syre, Oklahoma to go into the hardware business. Uncle Ernest stayed, trying with little success to make the farm work as best he could. Uncle Coke's family survived the worst of the Depression and the dust storms with the income from his rural mail route. However, when another man bid a lower rate for the job, Uncle Coke had no choice but to give up his farm and move to Plainview, Texas to look for work.

Uncle Boy sold his stations in Texola and moved to Clarendon, Texas to go into the wholesale gasoline business and to open a Phillips 66 station across from the courthouse and jail. Having retired, his dad and mother moved with him and Aunt Til. The old sheriff of Texola spent a lot of time at the station visiting with the retired sheriff of Clarendon and other old lawmen who lived in the area. For a while, Jean and I went to visit them during the summer. There wasn't much to do in Clarendon except sit in the station and listen to the old lawmen talk. I heard lots of stories—most of which I couldn't repeat to Mother or Dad. Sometimes when delivering gas to farms, Uncle Boy took me with him or I went to the movie downtown. I liked my Aunt and Uncle, but I preferred the time spent in Texola to Clarendon.

12 Junior High School

When I started the eighth grade—the first year in high school—I was thirteen years old, almost six feet tall, and weighed about 160 pounds. Prior to that year, I considered the relationship between education and me a draw. I did not have to work to get decent grades—at least grades high enough to keep Mother and Dad off my back—but school also cost me the chance to make more money by keeping me in school six hours per day.

To be honest, I did not care about school or grades. My teachers were so-so—none of them especially exciting or motivating. Most of my friends whose fathers worked for the railroad or were unemployed and trying to find work shared my feelings. Most kids went to school because it was expected, but the effort expended to learn depended upon having a future where education was important and would pay off in a job. My dad was my idol—people respected and liked him, and he provided for his family better than most in those days. Neither Mother nor Dad, having left to help on their fathers' farms, had gone to school at my age. I figured that I would eventually leave school and work with him on the railroad.

I knew I was as smart as any of my classmates—maybe even smarter than many of them if quickness is a sign of intelligence. I usually could figure out how things worked by watching them and I had a good memory—maybe not as good as Dad's, but better than most. What I lacked was knowledge—facts about history, science, and art—but useless knowledge was not appreciated. I wanted to learn what would make money for me, not how it could make me a better person and man. If there were do-overs in life, that is one mistake I would correct.

When I registered for classes that fall, it was my luck to have the assistant football coach for English. From my first day in class, he began to recruit me to play football because of my size. I was not interested since I was working every afternoon at Meacham's grocery store and had my paper route. Whether it was my lack of effort or his pettiness at my rejection of football, Coach McClure never gave me a passing grade on any assignment or test. That was the only class I failed that semester, but I figured I could make it up the following year without too much trouble, because my other grades were mostly Cs with a couple of Bs.

Bobby, my best friend from grade school, and I grew apart when we went into junior high school. We were still friends, but we did not share the same interests. He was mostly interested in music and ran around with kids who played in the band or sang in the choir. We usually walked to school together in the mornings, and then joined our separate groups of friends.

JM Simmons and Lindsey Swafford became my best running buddies. JM was my height, but quite a bit thinner. His thick black hair, unless smothered with hair oil, grew in every direction. He wore a perpetual smile and had a gift of gab—what some called a "smart mouth." His inability to keep his mouth shut got us in hot water plenty of times—especially when he was drinking beer—but he was solid as a rock when it came to friendship. He always had my back.

An Unsung Hero: Coming of Age in the Dust Bowl

Lindsey was shorter and younger than me, with a round face, light complexion, and dishwater blonde hair. He had thin lips that turned down at the corners, which made him look sour-pussed all of the time. However, his appearance disguised a sharp mind and a thoughtful personality. Lindsey did not talk much, but when he did, it seemed important. Of the three of us, Lindsey was the most popular with girls and other classmates. He was one of those people who made you feel good to be around him. We considered ourselves the Three Musketeers and were generally together when one of us was not working somewhere. All of us had part-time jobs where we earned extra money and best of all...Lindsey had access to his parents' car whenever he wanted it.

Boys and girls were just beginning to notice one another by the eighth grade—following the example of the older high school students. Mostly at that age, the genders stayed apart or met in groups where individuals could retreat into the safety of their friends if things got too uncomfortable or embarrassing. There were no parties except for dances at the school. Eighth graders usually did not attend. When they did, the younger boys gathered in groups to stand around and hold up the walls of the gymnasium. Sometimes, JM, Lindsey, and I met girls at the movies and sat with them, maybe holding hands, which caused everyone at school to declare the pair "boyfriend and girlfriend" the following Monday. I liked girls and they seemed to like me, but I was at a loss at how to proceed with a boy/girl relationship.

The summer after my eighth grade, I quit the paper route and found a job answering the phone for a cab company for one dollar a day. Dad was dickering to buy the company so he had no objections to me working there. He figured I could

120

keep him advised of their business. From my viewpoint, I was still in the big money. I went to work at six in the morning, finished at six in the evening, ate dinner at home, and met JM and Lindsey by seven thirty.

I discovered an added bonus when the drug store next door began giving punch cards to their customers. When the fifty-dollar card was filled with punches, the drugstore would exchange it for a diamond ring. At a nickel a punch, I knew it would take forever for me to fill the card. However, as with Dad's taxi company, a lot of my employer's business was delivering liquor around town for prescriptions. Whenever a call came in to deliver a pint, I asked the cab driver to use my punch card when he bought the liquor at the drug store. By the end of the summer, the card was full and I had a diamond ring. It was not much of a diamond, but Mother said it was the best ring she ever received. Dad just laughed.

The next year in the ninth grade, I went out for football. The head coach was my plane geometry teacher. The first semester, I made an A in geometry even though I did not understand many of the lessons. That semester was all about going to school classes and practicing football, hardly anything else. I was an offensive lineman, but I never played in the games. Every practice, a senior playing defense on the first team worked me over and I walked home after dark, too late and sore to go anywhere with my friends. In the meantime, JM and Lindsey were having a great time, still working in their part-time jobs and beginning to date the girls in our class using Lindsey's parents' car.

I finally turned in my football uniform and quit playing. The coach tried to convince me to stay on the team, promising me that "my time would come." Hoping Dad might make me

An Unsung Hero: Coming of Age in the Dust Bowl

play, the coach went to see him, but Dad told him it was my decision. The coach got even by failing me in plane geometry. I knew that protesting the grade was futile since I did not know anymore about plane geometry than I had when I joined the class. While having to repeat English had not bothered me too much, failing another class was serious. I knew I had to start studying so I could graduate with my friends.

That spring, the school required all students to take the Tuberculosis patch test. My arm swelled up after the test so I was sent to the doctor for an x-ray of my lungs. The Doctor's office was right above one of Dad's cabstands. He was old and his x-ray machine was old; he had one of Dad's cab drivers bring him fifty pounds of ice every day to put in the machine to cool it down. After he reviewed my x-ray, the doctor reported to the school and my parents that I had TB and would be sent to the Sanatorium in San Angelo for treatment as soon as he could get me in.

Tuberculosis (TB), commonly called "consumption," was a scary disease in the 1930s. It has been around humans forever. For centuries, people believed that vampires spread the disease—the first victim typically infecting other family members until the disease ran out of victims. Dr. Robert Koch identified a bacterium as the cause in 1882. Before a vaccine was developed, two out three people who got the disease died within a few years. There were no drugs to treat TB at that time, the first antibiotic developed in 1944. In 1938, the only treatment was bed rest and isolation; even then, one-half of the people entering a sanatorium died within five years after contracting the disease.

People were naturally afraid of tuberculosis since it was highly contagious—spread by inhaling a droplet from an infected person's cough, sneeze, speaking, singing, or spitting. Because of its virulence, the government ran an active campaign with posters in the schools and stores; movie newsreels warned about the danger of its spread by contact with a TB victim. I learned years later that scientists had developed a preventive vaccine in the 1920s, but it did not become widely available until after World War II. In 1939, few people, especially those living in a small town like Childress, had been vaccinated.

I suppose it is difficult to tell someone at any age that he has an incurable disease and will die in a short time. I learned about my condition from Mother and Dad after they talked to the Doctor. I will not ever forget that afternoon. Dad did not say much and had a hard time looking at me. He just sat there in our kitchen stone-faced, rubbing his thigh and smoking his pipe, seeming to catch his breath from time to time. Mother did all of the talking. She sat in one chair and I sat facing her in another. Both of my hands were clasped between her two hands. Tears ran down her face. She told me that I had TB and had to go to San Angelo for treatment. She told me that God loved me, He would take care of me, and they would visit me while I was there. Mother began sobbing. Dad stood up and held out his hand for me to shake. He just stood there with his eyes red-rimmed by his own tears and nodded his head as if to tell me everything would be all right.

I did not know what to think. Like everybody else, I had heard of tuberculosis, but did not know much about its symptoms or treatment. I supposed those who had it had difficulty breathing since it attacked the lungs. I did not have any problems breathing nor did I feel sick, so I had a hard time understanding the fuss. I could not imagine that anyone would make me leave home because I had a reaction to the skin test.

How could I be as healthy as a horse one day and ready to die the next? The diagnosis made no sense to me and I was sure the doctor would discover his mistake before anything drastic occurred.

In the meantime, the doctor restricted me to our house and would not allow me to go back to school. Since the school year was almost over, I got credit for the full year. Then my world began to turn upside down. I quickly learned that things would be different for me as well as the family.

Everyone in school and the neighborhood knew I had TB. Rumors and bad news travels fast in a small town…especially if it concerns someone dying. Most mothers, even those of my best friends and particularly if they had girls, did not want their kids to have anything to do with me. It was worse for Jean since some of her friends stopped playing with her because I was sick and their mothers were afraid that children around Jean would be exposed to the disease. I do not know how people treated Mother and Dad since they never said anything to me. I stopped going to church because of the possibility that I might infect someone. Dad pretty much stopped attending too, but Mother continued every Sunday morning and Wednesday evenings for prayers. She was determined that, if there were no other cure, prayer could save me.

Some of my classmates and so-called friends quit seeing me. However, although Bobby and I had not run together for years, he made the effort to come by the house every weekend to see if I needed anything. I wondered, had our roles had been reversed, would I have been as kind. I would like to think so, but I don't know.

JM and Lindsey treated me pretty much the same as before, as did a few girl friends from the neighborhood that I had known since grade school. Even after their mothers told them to stay away from me, they came by the house in the afternoons after school and talked to me about the happenings in town while we sat on my front porch. Even though I could not go to school, the doctor agreed to let me answer the phone for the cab company at night since I was the only one working in the office and the drivers could avoid me if I coughed.

13 The Sanatorium

It was almost three months before the sanatorium in San Angelo had an opening. Driving from Childress to San Angelo, more than 200 miles, took between five and six hours whether you went through Abilene or Sweetwater since there were no paved roads between the two towns. San Angelo is closer to central Texas, with even less rain and more heat than we had in Childress. The state of Texas built the sanatorium in the early 1900s. More than 500 patients were housed in the two-story brick dormitories with broad verandas when I arrived late in the summer of 1939. Residents lay on beds on the shaded porches when they were not in their dormitory beds.

My building had four sleeping sections—two upstairs and two downstairs—with twelve beds in each section. The entrance corridor and halls running the length of the building separated the four sections. Two nurses rotated in three shifts per day to cover the patients in each dormitory.

All ages—from 15 years old to 70 and older—resided in the dorm and I was the youngest in my section. Of course, men and women were housed in different dorms. In addition to the dorms, the campus included a building that functioned as a movie theatre during the week and a church on Sundays, a post office, a library, a barbershop, and a laundry in addition to the cafeteria where we ate our meals. Most of the residents were older men and women, but I saw kids as young as five or six years old who were there for treatment. There was a special dormitory and an elementary school for young kids, so I never got to know any of them. However, I met some of the other residents and even grew to like the place a little bit, but it was certainly not home.

My stay in San Angelo lasted a little over six months. I hated it at first and regularly wrote begging Mom and Dad to come and get me. I promised I would do anything if they would come after me. However, knowing that it was best for me to stay, Mother told me that coming home was not possible so I should try to make the best out of my situation. She encouraged me to go to the church and to pray every night, telling me that she said prayers for my cure constantly.

Mother and Dad tried to visit me every month, but sometimes due to bad weather, they could not make it. Mother wrote me every week and Jean sent pictures she drew in school. Because he was self-conscious about his handwriting, Dad never wrote, but sent his messages through Mother. A couple of my friends wrote the first month or so and I wrote back, but our letter writing petered out. I did not have anything to tell them about the sanatorium and I didn't care what was happening in high school.

Life in a sanatorium was different from life on the outside. Patients sometimes referred to the place as a "waiting room for death." Despite the staff's efforts to remain as cheerful as possible, a feeling of resignation and hopelessness was always present. There was laughter, muted generally, from time to time when someone noted the irony of the care provided to us compared to the economic hardships of most of our families living on the outside.

The rules forbade conversations about our conditions, symptoms, or death in an effort to keep everyone positive, but the nurses could not control every occasion when we talked. It

An Unsung Hero: Coming of Age in the Dust Bowl

was impossible not to think about tuberculosis or dying. We were all condemned, awaiting our execution just as surely as the murderer sitting on death row. The difference was that the prisoner knew the date of his last day on earth, while we lived each day never knowing when our moment would come.

In a place like San Angelo, residents do not make friends as people did outside the grounds. Being close to someone meant getting hurt when he left—either by discharge when he reached the maximum length of stay allowed, or death. Few patients actually died at the sanatorium. When a patient became too sick to follow the routine, he simply disappeared and another patient took his place; the previous resident either transferred to the San Angelo hospital or went home for his final hours.

The treatment for TB was complete bed rest since medical wisdom presumed any exercise would speed up "the end of many of those soon to be dead from tuberculosis." I spent most of the day and night in my bed or in a bed on one of the sleeping porches. The other patients called the bed rest "chasing," but I never figured out who, why, or what we were supposedly chasing. The nurses allowed us to get out of bed each morning at 7:00 AM after they took our temperatures.

Most days, I never got out of my pajamas and wore a housecoat and slippers wherever I went. Taking my clothes on and off several times a day did not make much sense, especially since I saw only the same people day after day. Sometimes on Saturdays, I took a bath and wore regular clothes to supper and then to church the next day just for a change. I only had one pair of pants, a single shirt, a couple of pairs of socks and underwear, and a pair of shoes. I had only a single small wooden box at the end of my bed in which to keep clothes or anything else.

The first job after I got out of bed each morning was to see the nurse down the hall that took my blood pressure, checked my pulse and directed me to the bathroom for a morning bowel movement. If everything went as expected, I joined the others to walk in a group to the cafeteria building for breakfast. I ate, sat outside on the porch and talked, and then returned to my bed at 9:00 AM.

At 11:30 AM, I repeated a similar routine of temperature and blood pressure checks followed by a meal and back to bed at 1:00 PM. I repeated the same procedure again at 5:00 PM, except that I could stay up after supper until 7:30 PM before going back to bed until the next morning. After I had been there a few weeks, I was allowed to stay up until 9:00 PM.

While in bed or "chasing," I could not talk, read, or listen to the radio. I just lay in bed, tried to keep quiet, and day dreamed about life after the sanatorium. Whenever someone violated a rule, they were "flattened" and lost their privilege to stay up until 9:00 PM for a while. If a patient was flattened, he could not go to the twice-weekly movies or church, which was the only time we saw girls or women.

Speaking to a girl was against the rules so we had to work out other ways of communicating. The building that served as the movie theatre and church separated the men and women dorms. Whenever the guys in my dorm knew the girls would be outside going to the movies or church, we would rush upstairs to sit at a window and write a single letter backwards on the glass pane with a crayon. When we knew the girls had read the letter, we wiped the pane with our handkerchiefs and wrote a second letter continuing until we spelled out a word. The messages were very short since it took only five or ten minutes to walk from the dorm to the movie theatre. Whenever it was the men's time to go to the show, the girls did the same thing from their dorm windows. It sounds innocent these days, but those times were the highlights of my week because I never saw a girl except for a middle-aged nurse.

Another way we talked to the girls was by "airplaning." I would write a note, fold it small enough to fit in an aspirin box, and sail the box to the girls while the preacher prayed and the nurses had their eyes closed with heads bowed. Some men could not take being apart from the women and slipped out at night to meet a girl from one of the dorms. If caught, they—man or woman, boy or girl—were sent home. I sometimes wonder why I never tried, since I wanted to go home so badly. I guess it was because I was in a routine to which I was accustomed and I did not think I had a choice. Looking back, I never met a single girl nor knew any of their names. I suspect none of the other fellows were any different. We were so lonely, missing girlfriends and mothers that even a long distance smile brightened our day and revived our spirits.

With all of the "chasing," I had a lot of time to think about my life, TB, and my future. I learned a lot about the disease from the other patients, especially that, even after the treatment, I was likely to die within a few years. It was funny, not "ha, ha" but odd, that I never felt sick and never had trouble with my breathing. More surprisingly, I got bigger and, I think, stronger while I was there. It was hard to believe I had an assassin inside me that was certain to kill me before my time.

William M. Forsythe

I do not remember being afraid of dying. I did not have any great dreams to fulfill, adventures to seek, or ambitions to accomplish. I had not thought much about my future before the sanatorium. I guessed that I would grow up, get married, work on the railroad like Dad, worry about paying bills, and try to be a good husband and father. My expected future was not especially exciting or extraordinary. I did not look forward to becoming an adult with responsibilities, but I was not afraid of my future either.

I had watched the adults in my life constantly worry and work to keep food on the table and a roof over their heads. In the midst of the Depression and then the dust storms, few people smiled or had many occasions of fun. As Brother Grey preached in church, my family and I believed that true happiness came when we got to heaven. This life was a test to see if His disciples could and would follow His commandments. Dying young meant my test would be shorter than most.

I believed I had been a good boy and son. I had never gotten into real trouble—at most doing stupid pranks with the other kids in my neighborhood. I never stole anything and I didn't lie much except for an occasional fib. I worked hard and did my chores without complaint. I did not hate anyone and no one, as far as I knew, hated me. I loved my Mother, Father, and Jean. I never took God's name in vain and I knew nothing about fornication or adultery. I figured I was in good shape to go to heaven since I was baptized and went to church regularly. I knew I did not pray as much as I should have and I had only confessed and repented the one time when I got baptized. At age fourteen, most people have had little chance to be truly evil or even bad—at least, I had not.

I spent Thanksgiving and Christmas in San Angelo before going home to Childress. When Mom and Dad picked me up to go home, it was too late in the second semester to start school. We did not talk much on the way home. What was there to say? No one knew whether I was cured or if the disease was just waiting to strike when things were going well.

I had not felt ill since the day of the patch test. Not a day between the test and going to the sanatorium! Not a day at the sanatorium! Never! I did not know what to expect or when my symptoms would appear. I knew I was sick and likely to die within the next five years; the doctors at the sanatorium explained the disease and other patients told of people who had died at the sanatorium. "Maybe," I thought, "I'll go to bed one night and not wake up the next morning."

14 Homecoming

The day after we returned to Childress, Mother fixed a special supper for me as if it were Christmas or Thanksgiving. There were just the four of us—Mother, Dad, Jean and me. Jean wondered if I was different and didn't know how to treat me. She was about ten and had learned more about tuberculosis since I had left home. Her peers had treated her poorly during the three months before I went to the sanatorium. Their parents and other adults had not said much to Mother or Dad, but stayed away because they feared being infected. As time went by and I was absent, their panic abated. However, little kids are different—whether intentionally cruel or just dumb—they repeat things their parents think or say in private.

While I was away, Jean's relationship with her friends and schoolmates had recovered to my pre-TB days, probably because no one else in the family got sick. I know she loved me, as much as a younger sister can love a brother, but she worried her classmates would again exclude her, especially when the neighbors realized I had returned. Since I had not been "cured," no one could say anything to allay her concern. All of us were entering uncharted territory.

During my freshman or sophomore year, I read the book "The Scarlet Letter" in English class. The book tells the story of a Puritan woman in the 1600s that was guilty of adultery. Her punishment required she wear a big red letter "A" on her dress so everyone would know of her sin and shame. Like many in my class, the idea of adultery captured my attention, rather than the punishment. I learned over the next two years that the people in Childress had affixed the letters "TB" to my chest just as visibly as the citizens of Boston had branded Hester Prynne with the letter "A" 500 years before.

I could not go back to school because I was too far behind to catch up during the remaining semester. So, I went back to answering the phone for Dad's cab company. I worked during the day when school was open and switched to nights that summer. My friends, JM and Lindsey, treated me as if I had never left, other than teasing me about being a year behind them in school. I discovered that, with the freedom of Lindsey's car, they had also started drinking.

While my parents disapproved of alcohol, I had no strong feelings about it. When JM offered me a beer the first time, I did not hesitate. I discovered that drinking made me feel better—not when I got drunk, but when I found just a little buzz to relax me. I started smoking cigarettes too, even though smoking was supposed to be harmful for a TB victim. I figured I had nothing to lose—so I tried smoking and liked it. I hid my drinking from Mom and Dad, but not my smoking. Although Mother warned me that I was hurting myself with my bad lungs, she never forbade me to smoke. I think she thought as the doctors told her that the damage to my lungs from tuberculosis had already occurred and scolding me would not make me better.

Despite my hope for a fresh start when school opened, my reputation as a TB carrier stuck with me. Some people did not want to have anything to do with me, and others—including some teachers—treated me with pity as if I might pass away at any moment. On the other hand, nobody, even Mother and Dad, expected much from me. I think they thought I was entitled to as much happiness as I could get if I was going to die within a few years…that meant hiding their disappointments and expectations for me.

For a while, I relished the freedom and considered it compensation for the time I had spent in the sanatorium. I realized years later that it was a mistake on their part and mine. Since no one expected anything of me, I lost any sense of pride in my accomplishments; whatever I did had no value for anyone, including me. Even worse, I lost confidence in myself. I was no longer Jimmy Lewis, Lardy's boy who worked at the cab company, but instead, "Jimmy Lewis, the poor boy who has TB. Let's be nice to him because his life will be short."

Because of the year I spent out of school, my friends were in the class ahead of me and there was no way I could catch them. They were seniors having completed their junior year, the 10th grade, during the year I was confined. I still had classes to make up from my sophomore year in addition to the year I lost to the TB. I was in classes with people a year or more younger than I, and it was embarrassing. In addition, everyone knew I had been in the sanatorium and many feared I might infect them. JM, Lindsey, and the few former classmates who were not afraid, were in other classes. I felt friendless and alone, so I sat in the back of the classroom feeling sorry for myself.

Although I am not proud of it, I allowed self-pity to separate me from my classmates—my fault, not theirs. I developed a bad inferiority complex and lost any remaining interest in school that I might have had before the sanatorium. In fact, I was not interested in very much of anything. Though I stayed in school for the remainder of that year and the next, my grades were poor and I failed biology. To compensate for

An Unsung Hero: Coming of Age in the Dust Bowl

my self-consciousness, I became the class clown, often making myself the butt of my own jokes. My teachers hated that—whether because of what I said about myself or because I disrupted the class, or, perhaps, because they thought of me as a walking corpse. I don't know.

William M. Forsythe

15 World War II Begins

Roosevelt initiated program after program to help people survive the Depression and the ravages in the Dust Bowl, but the hostilities in Europe were the real impetus for economic improvement; the war created a new market for American goods. Factories called back furloughed employees, and railroad traffic got much busier, which required new tracks and more trains to handle the goods and people moving around the country. While the economy improved and men returned to work, the declaration of war in 1941 spurred full employment and the end of programs like the Civilian Conservation Corps.

Factories quit manufacturing civilian goods in order to manufacture products for the war. No one could buy cars, furniture, liquor, tobacco, houses, or clothes. For the average American, necessities were scarce and luxuries were non-existent. The government rationed food, gas, and other staples through government stamps distributed once a month at the Post Office. When I went to the store or to the gas station, I could only buy the goods for which I had stamps—no stamps, no purchases. Stickers were attached to automobile windshields to show the number of gallons allotted for that car per month. Across the U.S, speed limits were reduced to 35 miles an hour to conserve gasoline.

Even though prices of most goods were frozen, unscrupulous merchants found ways around the limits. For example, some liquor stores required an additional purchase of a bottle of rum or gin in order to purchase a bottle of whiskey.

An Unsung Hero: Coming of Age in the Dust Bowl

While technically within the law, most people considered the practice unethical and taking advantage of the situation, but there was no choice if you wanted whiskey. About this time, distillers began to sell whiskey and other spirits in four-fifth of a quart bottles instead of full quarts, even though the smaller bottles sold for the same price as the quarts. Buyers referred to the new bottles as "four-fifths," eventually shortening the name to "fifths," the term we use today.

Automobile manufacturers stopped the production of new cars and began making war materials. The government set maximum prices for used cars available from the dealers and car lots. To avoid the ceiling price, some unethical dealers required their prospective customer to put $50 or $100 of cash in an old billfold and drop it somewhere on the lot where the dealer could find it. When the dealer found the billfold with the money, the customer could buy the car at the ceiling price.

The Government also taxed cosmetics.

Manufacturers used silk as a component of some war materials, so popular silk hosiery was unavailable. Trying to imitate the appearance of wearing hose, women resorted to dying their legs and drawing a thin, black line down the center back of thigh and calf. Believe me, it is not easy to draw a straight line down a soft leg as I discovered while trying to help my cousin Addie Ruth paint her legs. Even so, despite the difficulty, some girls continued the practice for years.

On Pearl Harbor day—December 7, 1941—I was in my junior year of school in Childress. Everyone knew the war was inevitable, but did not know when or how it might start. There was a lot of sentiment to stay out of the European war, particularly in the community around North Texas. However, the surprise attack changed everyone's opinion. Many young men volunteered immediately for the service. JM and his older brother, Ray, signed up and left Childress just a few months after the attack.

I had mixed feelings about the war, though I knew I would never be in the service. Because of the tuberculosis, I was sure to be medically unfit. It seemed shameful that I could not fight since I had nothing to lose by going to war. I expected to die in a hospital bed from consumption within a few years anyway.

The war changed the attitude of my friends almost immediately. As young men, they knew the probability of being drafted into the service was very high and, when it happened, there was the possibility they would never come home. Like me, they felt the need to experience as much as possible in the time they had left—even if the activity was a little dangerous and outside the approval of our parents. With JM gone, the four of us—Lindsey, Roy Simmons, and Charles Yeary—often drove to Hollis, Oklahoma to buy beer and occasionally double-dated. Most of my dates were not romances because the girls in Childress, knowing about the TB, did not consider me much of a catch since a long-term relationship ending with marriage was out of the question.

One afternoon in the spring, I skipped school to meet Lindsey for a trip to Amarillo, the biggest city in the Panhandle with "bright lights, loose women, and cheap whiskey." In Lindsey's car, Lindsey, Roy, and I picked up Charles in Memphis, and headed west to Amarillo. Charles and Lindsey worked for a cigarette company that serviced accounts throughout the Panhandle. Charles had been working his route and had $800 in collections to turn into his company

An Unsung Hero: Coming of Age in the Dust Bowl

when we returned to Childress. We continued and had some fun, drinking beer and talking to the "professional" women that flourished in the big town. I also bought a couple of pints of whiskey for a friend in Childress.

On the way home, Roy and I went to sleep in the back seat. Charles was driving and ran out of gas near Clarendon, so he and Lindsey left us asleep and took off walking to buy gas. As luck would have it, a highway patrol officer stopped when he saw the car parked beside the highway. He found us asleep with the whiskey in the seat beside us. The officer arrested Roy and me and put us in handcuffs in the backseat of his car. As we were driving away, we passed Lindsey and Charles walking back to the car with the gas. He stopped, handcuffed them, and drove the four of us to Clarendon where we spent the rest of the night in jail.

While checking us into the jail, the police found the $800 that Charles was carrying to give to the company. They immediately suspected the money had been stolen despite Charles' protestations and explanation. Fortunately, no one had reported a robbery so we were cleared of that charge. The next morning without allowing us make a phone call, the police marched us to court before an old judge.

The Judge told us we could plead guilty to being drunk and pay a twelve-dollar fine or go back to jail until trial later in the spring. Since I was eighteen, I pled guilty and called Uncle Boy to pay my fine. Roy was twenty-one and claimed he had been asleep, not drunk, so they let him go. Charles pled guilty, too, and paid the twelve-dollar fine from the eight hundred dollars of company money from the cigarette route. Since it was his car, the sheriff charged Lindsey with

William M. Forsythe

"transporting liquor"—a more serious crime; he pled "not guilty" and went back to jail.

When Uncle Boy showed up to pay my fine, he chewed out the sheriff, a friend of his, for refusing to let me call him before we went to court. Uncle Boy was angry because he could have gotten us released without any fine or charge if the sheriff had called him. The sheriff had intended to impound Lindsey's car, but Uncle Boy talked him into letting me drive it back to Childress—probably because the sheriff knew there would be hell to pay with Uncle Boy if he had not released the car.

The following day, Lindsey's parents went to Clarendon and paid Lindsey's one hundred dollar fine. Lindsey initially refused to let them pay it, determined that he would work it off in jail time, but finally relented when his mother started crying. That weekend, the report of our arrest with all of the details was in the Sunday papers. Charles swore he would never go back to Clarendon again, but settled for not stopping in the town on future trips. I was the only one of the four of us still in school, but I figured, "After TB, what's a little jail time?" When anyone asked me about it, I just laughed and said, "Our next party will be dry."

The arrest was bad enough, but having the arrest reported in the newspaper was worse. Dad was disgusted and told me in no uncertain terms that if it happened again, I needed to find a new place to live. Mother's reaction was worse—she cried and told me that while she would always love me, she was ashamed of me. Jean just looked at me, knowing that she would have to face more scorn from her friends about her brother. I realized that I had not considered my family's feelings or the toll on them since I had come home from the sanatorium. I promised Mother that I would try to do better in the future and swore, no matter what, that I would never be arrested again.

Apparently, Mother and Dad had been considering our situation in Childress for some time. With Dad's seniority, he could transfer to Amarillo or Wichita Falls without losing any income. He would need to sell the cab company and other businesses, but felt that he could easily find a buyer. Jean was ready to start her first year in high school, so a move then would be less traumatic than waiting a year or more. Most importantly, a new town where no one knew about my TB would give each of us a new start.

My best friends had graduated and either enlisted in the service or were whiling away time until they were drafted, so I had nothing in Childress to keep me. Despite having tuberculosis, my health was good. I was stronger than I had ever been and could work all day without problems. Best of all, no one in our new town would know about my history. I thought I could finally date a girl without her being afraid I would infect her or wanting to make me a "best friend" because I was not marriage material.

The day we moved to Wichita Falls right after school closed in the spring of 1942. That move was one of the happiest days of my life.

William M. Forsythe

16 Wichita Falls

Contact with my uncles' families grew more infrequent with the start of the war. Uncle Homer and Uncle Coke had moved away from Texola—Uncle Homer to Syre, Oklahoma with a hardware business and Uncle Coke to Plainview to open a self-service laundry. Uncle Ernest registered as a Conscientious Objector when the war started and tried to keep farming. The Government drafted and assigned him to work in the beet fields of Michigan for the war's duration. He let the bank have his farm, moved to Michigan, married, and never came back to Texas.

During the summer of 1942 when we moved to Wichita Falls, I found work building the new Air Force base in Frederick, Oklahoma. Uncle Homer had previously sold his hardware store in Syre, Oklahoma to open a new store in Tipton, Oklahoma, about fifteen miles from Frederick. I stayed with them for the summer and went back and forth to work with Lura Fay and Addie Ruth. Addie Ruth worked on the base and Lura worked at the courthouse in downtown Frederick. The three of us paid another fellow, who had a car and worked construction with me, to take us to and from work each day.

Aunt Edna cooked meals in the kitchen in the rear of the store and the four Forsyths slept in two upstairs bedrooms. I slept on a cot in the downstairs storeroom. My job carrying lumber for the head carpenter paid thirty cents per hour in cash every week with twenty percent of the total wages deducted for taxes to pay for the war. On the weekends, I hung around with Lura, Addie Ruth, and two of their girl friends, mostly playing tennis.

That summer, Addie Ruth, not being able to buy hose and tired of shaving, decided that she would have me pull the hair on her legs, with the expectation that the hairs would not grow back. She stood on one chair while I sat on another with a pair of tweezers in one hand and a magnifying glass in the other to see the light, almost invisible, individual hairs. Every time I pulled a hair, she yelped and complained that I hurt her. I could not keep from laughing which made her even angrier. After about fifteen minutes of my snickering with her swatting my head each time I snorted, I had a clear spot about the size of a quarter. When she looked down and realized how much work remained, she said, "That's it. I can't stand any more of this."

After shaving and dyeing her legs, later that day she asked me to paint the black seams down the back of her legs to look like she was wearing real silk hose. She hopped up on the chair and handed me a black marker with instructions to draw the line straight down the center of each leg. I tried, but the line wavered from side to side from her thigh to her heel. When she looked down at the results, she screamed and hit me on the head again, thus ending my first and last opportunity to develop a new skill as a cosmetologist. That was our last summer together. Addie Ruth was the greatest friend I ever had and our friendship never faded in the years to come.

After moving to Wichita Falls, I had no intention of finishing high school. I still lacked more than a year of the courses needed to graduate. Older people at the time generally lacked high school degrees, but it did not seem to hinder them finding work. I knew I was not cut out to be a salesman or sit in an office. I wanted to be outside or doing work where I used my hands with my brain—physically touching the tools, equipment, and the products of my work.

When I told the folks I was not going back to school, Mother cried and Dad was heart-broken. If I graduated, I would be the first in my family to have a high school degree. Dad's attitude about education had undergone a 180-degree reversal in the previous five years, partly because he felt I, being a tuberculosis victim, would be unable to find or handle a physically taxing job. He thought having a high school degree might give me an advantage in the work force.

Feeling guilty because I had caused them so much worry over the years, I agreed to try school one more year. If I could graduate in that time, great; if not, I had shown them that I tried. The school records transferred from Childress included the year I lost due to the sanatorium stay. Luckily, the high school counselor was sympathetic to my situation and agreed to allow me take two English courses and six other subjects each semester. I quit my job in Frederick and moved to Wichita to begin my senior year in the fall of 1942.

When I had turned 18 the previous spring, I registered for the military draft as required by Federal law. Shortly after school started that fall, I received a notice to report for a physical. Upon arriving at the facility with about 100 other young men, I completed a form that included my medical history and the stay in the San Angelo sanatorium. The physical exam also included an X-ray of my chest. Later the same day, a nurse found me in a group waiting for another procedure and took me back for a second X-ray.

Oh, no, I thought. *The TB must have gotten worse. I'm not going back to a sanatorium. I'd rather go to the front lines than go through that again!*

For the rest of the day, all I could think about was the stay in San Angelo. I really hated it—the loneliness, the isolation, and just killing time day after day. When the doctor called me to his office late in the afternoon, I prepared myself as best I could for the bad news.

The doctor was middle-aged, balding with just a fringe of hair running around the back of his head from ear to ear, wearing rimless glasses. The nurse took me into his office and told me to sit in one of the wooden chairs in front of his desk. I sat there, silent, and waited until he looked up from the papers he had been reading and said, "It says here that you were a resident of the San Angelo Tuberculosis Sanatorium in 1938."

"Yes, sir. I was there from September 1938 until March 1939."

"Why were you sent there?" he asked.

"I had tuberculosis and San Angelo was the closest sanatorium to my home town, Childress," I replied, wondering where this conversation was going. It was not what I expected to hear.

The doctor looked down at his paper and back at me, then asked, "Who sent you there?"

"The doctor in Childress who works with the school. My patch test was bad, so he took an X-ray and told us I had TB. I had to wait almost four months before going to San Angelo."

William M. Forsythe

"What do you know about tuberculosis?"

"Just what the doctors told me, and my parents, and what I heard from the other patients. I know that most people die within five years after getting it. It's been almost five years now for me. Are you going to tell me I'm dying?" I asked, leaning forward in my chair to stare at him.

The doctor looked at me, and then looked down at the report he was holding. "How do you feel?" he asked.

"I've always felt fine and I haven't even been sick with a cold for a long time. I feel the same as I did before I went to San Angelo, the same way I've felt for the last three years. Has something happened? Are my X-rays worse?"

I was getting mad because the doctor was dragging out the news. I was ready for him to tell me that my time had finally come and he was messing around. *I'm the guy with the disease. Why can't you tell me the bad news straight out and be done with it?*

The doc put the report down, took off his glasses with his left hand, and with eyes closed, began to rub the bridge of his nose between the thumb and forefinger of his right hand. After a moment that seemed like an hour, he replaced his glasses, opened his eyes, stretched both hands, and clasped them together in front of him on the desk.

"Son, I don't know how to tell you, but you do not have tuberculosis. From the x-rays I've reviewed, you never had tuberculosis. I don't know why you were told that you had TB or why you were sent to San Angelo."

I sat up straight in my chair as if he had slapped me. I was stunned. *I don't have tuberculosis*, I thought. *Damn, you're kidding me. I don't have tuberculosis! I've never had tuberculosis!* I slumped back in my chair, not knowing what to say. I thought of how Mother and Dad would react when they heard the news. Would they be happy knowing I wasn't going to die? Or maybe they would be angry, because of living through three years of worry for nothing, of having to sell their house, and of moving to Wichita Falls just to escape the small town prejudice and fears of Childress?

Jumbled thoughts flew through my mind…another one beginning before the first completed. Memories of the girls who wouldn't date me or insisted that we "just be friends' because of the TB clashed with images of Mother crying when she told me I had tuberculosis and Jean looking at me when her friends' mothers quit inviting her to play with their daughters.

The doctor picked up his fountain pen and began to write on the report. "I don't know what happened or why, so I can't do anything about it. I can see on my records that the misdiagnosis cost you a year of school and that you are currently a senior at Wichita Falls High School. You will be classified 1-A as the result of this physical, but I am going to recommend a one-year deferment so you can get your degree before you might be called up."

After signing his name on the report, the doctor stood up, leaned across the desk and extended his right hand. "Good luck, Mr. Lewis."

I scrambled out of my seat as the nurse opened the door and shook his hand. I did not know what to say. I felt like laughing and crying at the same time. I was excited to have a future that I had not expected and I was relieved that Death was going to have to wait at least a little time longer than he expected.

ABOUT THE AUTHOR

William M. Forsythe is a retired senior business executive and relative of Jimmy Ray Lewis. He was born and lived in Wichita Falls, Texas where he graduated from high school and attended Midwestern University. After a forty-year career as a small business owner, he retired and began writing. This is his first biography.

Read on for an excerpt from
William M. Forsythe's

An Unsung Hero: Sniper's Target

Chapter 1

As I sat on the train from Dallas, Texas to Little Rock, Arkansas listening to the conversations around me, I realized none of us knew what to expect when we got to our destination and thereafter. My companions and I—mostly young men between the ages of 18 and 25 with a few gray-haired men scattered among us—were draftees into the United States Army—new bodies to replace casualties of wars half-way around the world. The United States and its allies had fought their way onto the shores of France with an estimated 10,000 dead and wounded the month before. While a start on the road to victory, everyone recognized the battle was just beginning.

The Germans were a lethal fighting force that had honed their military skills for five years conquering countries in Europe. Their major ally, Japan, controlled much of the South Pacific including the Philippines and had drawn America into the conflict with their dastardly attack on Pearl Harbor. They seemed determined to win at any cost in lives of their own people or their enemies. Looking around the train compartment, I realized that some of us would not be coming back from the war and others would return with arms and legs missing. It was a sobering thought that evening of July 14, 1944.

Like the others, I received notice to report to the San Antonio Induction Center where I boarded a train to Camp Robinson near Little Rock, Arkansas. It was my first trip beyond the borders of Texas—I do not count Oklahoma, since it is just a little brother of the Lone Star state. Before the draft,

I worked for almost a year on the railroad, riding freight trains throughout the hot, dusty plains of the Panhandle of Texas. At age 20, I had never traveled east of Dallas.

As we click-clacked over the rails through east Texas and southern Arkansas, I wondered why my ancestors had left the forest-filled valleys of Tennessee to move west during the previous century. In my part of Texas, temperatures regularly soared over 100 degrees in the summer and early fall. West Texas is a region populated with patches of mesquite trees, sagebrush, and burned-out indiangrass. Whirring grasshoppers as long as your finger rise suddenly to the sky; horny toads— descendants of the dinosaurs—feed on colonies of inch-long red ants; and rattle snakes grow thicker than a grown man's arm. Some say a tall man can see the buildings of Amarillo from the 125 miles distant town of Lubbock with only a few trees to obstruct his view. The tall trees, green grasses, hills, and valleys that flashed by the windows of our east-bound train seemed to be an Eden. I promised myself that, if I did return, I would explore America and see the "amber waves of grain" and "purple mountains majesties" described in the songs of my childhood.

When we arrived at Little Rock depot, khaki-clad, bellowing soldiers hustled us off the train into waiting buses for the short trip to Camp Robinson. At the camp, everything happened in a blur. Despite the chaos and confusion, we quickly learned to form lines by the first letter of our last names. In short order, we were assigned barracks and issued clothing and boots. To my surprise, everything for me was a good fit. I do not know if everyone had the same luck, but no one complained.

After being outfitted and settled in, we lined up in rows to see an officer dentist and his assistant. When the dentist stopped in front of me, I opened my mouth wide so he could inspect my teeth. He poked around with his little steel probe, ignoring whenever I winced, and told his assistant what I needed. The assistant leaned over, looked at my dog tags, wrote everything on his clipboard, and moved to the next man in line. Neither the dentist nor his assistant spoke a word to me, not even "thank you" when they were done.

About a week later, my instructor directed me to the dental clinic, an almost perfect replica of the barbershop where military barbers buzz-cut our hair the first day. Instead of barber chairs, dental chairs lined the hall with wooden benches for those waiting. I had never visited a dentist while growing up—instead followed Mother's instructions to brush my teeth morning and evening for dental hygiene—so the experience was new and a little frightening to me. Soldiers up and down the line of dental chairs were moaning in pain and spitting blood as the dentists did their work. As quickly as one patient was done, the next soldier rose from the bench, took his place in the chair, and everyone slid over to the adjacent spot on the bench.

Dentistry as practiced by the Army was straight-forward—every person was treated on the assembly line with the dentist doing whatever work was needed all at one time. If the recruit needed a tooth pulled and five fillings—or a dozen—the dentist treated him in one sitting with minimal use of Novocaine to dull any pain. I think the Army believed that pain and haste made good partners, the latter reducing the former.

From my seat on the bench I had the perfect view of a mighty struggle of a short, wiry dentist as he tried to pull a lower tooth from the mouth of a large, barrel-chested recruit. Standing beside the chair, the dentist clamped both hands around a small set of pliers—the tooth puller—buried in the reluctant recruit's mouth. He strained and strained—the muscles in his forearms popping with his effort—but got nowhere with the tooth. He began to curse. His patient squirmed in the chair, but there was no retreat. Disgusted, the dentist climbed into the patient's lap, straddling both legs to get better leverage. Suddenly, a loud crack pierced the din of moans and curse words. The guy screamed, knocked the dentist away, and jumped out of the chair. Before anything else could happen, two soldiers grabbed the moaning patient and hustled him out of the room.

To my horror, the assistant called out, "Lewis!" Let me tell you, I was not anxious to be next, but was given no choice. Determined not to show my fear and consternation, I shuffled over, sat down, and grabbed the arms of the chair. The dentist, silently motioned for me to open my mouth. Suddenly, he stopped and said, "I just broke a guy's jaw. I'm in no shape to work on you. You can leave and we will call you." I left.

On my second visit a few days later, the dentist said that while I didn't need any fillings, he wanted to pull a crooked tooth on one side of my jaw to avoid problems later. My entreaties to keep the tooth were ignored and left me with one less tooth and a sore mouth.

The 270 trainees in my group came from across the United States. I met fast talking people with thick accents and unpronounceable names. I had better luck understanding my Mexican friends speaking Spanish than those from New York. Our training unit included college graduates and high school dropouts, but people generally got along once the pecking order was sorted out.

In almost every crowd, there is a bully who thinks he can run over everybody. Our unit was no different. We had a few guys who tried to intimidate others with their aggression. They instinctively knew the weak, the unsure, and anyone who might be cowed physically.

I had learned to deal with bullies when my family moved from Childress to Wichita Falls before my senior year of high school. Because the new guy is always a target, I wore a bull's eye in Wichita.

During high school, people generally left me alone because I was bigger than most and avoided places where trouble was likely. However, one Saturday night below the dam at Lake Wichita, a friend and I were leaning on his car, drinking beer, smoking, and talking. Another car pulled up beside us with a bunch of drunken football players from school. I recognized one of them from a class we shared.

Butch Nemi was about my height, but outweighed me by fifty pounds. He was one of those people who demand to be the center of attention—the guy who whispers off-color remarks in class with a demeaning nickname for everyone. I had never talked to him before that night and I did not know any of his hangers-on. As they climbed out of their car, I looked over, nodded hello, and turned back to my friend.

"Hey, buddy, I hear you're looking for me." I turned around to see Butch walking toward me with a big grin on his face with the four other boys in a snickering and laughing semi-circle behind him. They had seen this act before.

"No, I'm not looking for you. I don't even know you. We don't want any trouble. Why don't you guys have a beer and go on to town?"

"My girlfriend, Judy, said you were looking for me. Are you calling her a liar?" He turned to grin at his friends, thinking he had me in a no-win situation. If I said his girlfriend was not a liar, he would accuse me of calling him a liar. Either answer would provoke an assault.

As he turned back toward me, I hit him with a right cross, splitting his left eyebrow that started streaming blood. He fell backward into his buddies and landed on his butt with blood running down his face onto the front of his shirt. I stepped up and kicked him hard in the side two or three times. He rolled over on his stomach and began to throw up with no fight left in him.

The confrontation from his first comment to the end lasted less than ten seconds. With my fists still raised, I backed away watching his buddies in case any of them felt they needed to defend him. No one did.

"I told you I didn't want any trouble. I told you to go on. But you didn't listen," I said with the adrenaline still spiking in my body. "You better remember this: Do not mess with me! Bother me again and I will hurt you bad." I took a breath, trying to calm down. "Now get his butt out of here."

Without saying anything, his four buddies scrambled to help him into the car and drove away.

During the fracas, my friend had not said anything. I stepped back to the car, took a swallow of beer, and lit a cigarette.

"Wow, I wasn't expecting that." He looked at me with a new respect. "Where did you learn to fight?"

"I'm not a fighter. I don't like bullies. As far as I'm concerned, it is over. The guy just poked his stick in the wrong hole."

We drank a couple more beers and went home. Still revved up from the fight, I played the scene over and over in my mind when I went to bed. It was my first real fight. My friends and I had scuffled around and wrestled some in Childress, but nothing serious. Adolescent head-butting usually begins in junior high along with acne, a deeper voice, and body hair—evidence of an over-abundance of testosterone. Having been diagnosed with tuberculosis and left alone because no one wanted to be infected, I had not been a part of establishing my place in the young male pecking order during those years.

As I thought about the evening, I realized I owed Butch a big favor. His willingness to fight me was a sign that neither he nor his friends knew anything about my TB history. If he didn't know about it, no one else was likely to know. For the first time since junior high school, I was like everyone else.

By the following Monday, the story was all over school. I did not mind since a reputation of being tough discouraged other want-to-be tough guys and bullies from testing me. Our confrontation certainly helped my popularity among my classmates, especially some of the girls who had ignored me before. I discovered that Butch had a reputation as one of the tougher guys in town, probably because he was a bully. He may have been tough, but he never had a chance to get going that night. It was more luck on my part than skill, but I willingly accepted my new mantle as a "tough guy."

Butch and I never spoke to each other again, even after high school. I think he was drafted and never came back to Wichita. In any event, the fight—if you call it that—cemented my own reputation as someone to be left alone and I never had another problem in school. It was also a lesson I carried the rest of my life: acting tough is almost as good as being tough when confronting a bully.

Group living was another issue some of the men in our training unit had never encountered before the Army. The lack of privacy was new and occasionally resulted in dust-ups when someone got their nose out of joint. When I was fourteen, I spent over six months living in a tuberculosis sanatorium with other boys and men. As a consequence, I was a private person—slow to warm up to others until I got to know them. I knew that a sense of privacy was mental, not physical, and the best protection of your own personal space was setting the lines by acts, not words. Having suffered the ostracism of my high school classmates and hometown due to my status as a tuberculosis carrier, I was also used to being on my own. Even though the Army declared the diagnosis a mistake and drafted me to soldier, I had already built mental and psychological walls to protect myself. These barriers were not easily abandoned with strangers.

Especially with easier victims around, my attitude combined with body build discouraged those who might have been tempted to bully me. In my experience, most people quickly learn to respect the limits of other people, especially if there are consequences to those who test the boundaries. I made a few friends, no obvious enemies, and generally got along with everyone during our sixteen-week training period.

As replacements for units already in the field, none of us knew where we might be assigned. Almost everyone hoped to go fight the Nazis in Europe and let others fight the Japanese. Most of us had never seen a Japanese person or knew much about their culture. Our knowledge came almost totally from the war propaganda films that depicted them as smiling, squint-eyed sub-humans with thick glasses. We thought them somewhat cowardly due to their sneak attack on Pearl Harbor, but thoroughly evil and capable of any atrocity. At that time in our training, many of us believed there was some honor in war, and that Americans were different than the soldiers on the other side who were naturally treacherous and would torture, rape, and murder without qualm.

I had a personal fear of being sent to the Pacific to fight on islands with poisonous snakes and insects in addition to the human enemies. The Japanese were short, probably under five-foot six-inches tall. I was almost six-foot three-inches. That difference was a big advantage in target size. Because my knowledge came only from conversations with Dad who fought in World War I and watching the *Sergeant York* movie, I did not know what kind of fighting we would be doing. A potential Japanese adversary would have the additional benefit of being able to hide behind smaller cover. From the little I knew from the newsreels, the Germans did not appear physically different from me, so the fight seemed a little fairer.

My time in Little Rock wasn't too bad. Basic training consisted of short hikes, close order drill, and longer hikes. For some of the nine-mile hikes, we alternated walking and jogging fifty steps at a time to quickly cover as much ground as possible. This drill—what our instructors called "forced marches"—would be necessary when another outfit was in trouble and needed help. Calisthenics, tours through the obstacles courses, and hand-to-hand combat practice filled the time between marches. A couple of weeks into the training, we were issued M-1 rifles and taught to shoot. I had done some hunting growing up, so guns were not new to me. The M-1 weighed about ten pounds, but seemed a lot heavier when you carried it all day with a full pack.

At the end of six weeks, a two-day pass was given to all recruits. My wife, Velta, came to Little Rock for the weekend. We had been married less than a year when I was called up.

We had met in high school while both seniors, even though she was two years younger than me. I first saw her while waiting on the corner for the school bus. She and another girl walked up and stopped near the back of the line. The two stood apart from the others, laughing and giggling, while I tried not to be obvious in staring at her. She was movie-star pretty with her long curly black hair brushing her shoulders and framing her face. Her rimless glasses magnified her dark brown—almost black—eyes and long lashes.

I would really like to meet her, I thought. I guess I was staring because she suddenly looked at me and winked. I could not think of anything smart to say before the bus pulled up and people crowded past me to load. Like a gentleman, I stood aside while she and her friend boarded the bus. I noticed she was just at my eye level when she stood on the first step. I hoped I might find a seat near her and introduce myself. However, the two girls found the last seats near the front while I had to go on to the back. Each time the bus stopped, more kids got on, shoving me farther away from my prize. By the time I got off at school, she and her friend had disappeared. I looked for her over the next few days, but never saw her. Being the first girl who had ever winked at me, she was hard to forget.

One afternoon, a couple of weeks later, I was surprised to see her with my friend, Lindale. They had skipped school and gone horseback riding. The following week, I ran into her and a couple of her girlfriends at the downtown skating rink. She was a terrific skater and a sight on the rink. Since I had done most of my skating on rough concrete sidewalks, my skills on an indoor rink were limited. I could skate fast, but skating backward or twirling was out of my league. We skated as a couple a few times, but she did not seem to be impressed with my flare. When I finally got the courage to ask her about Lindale, she told me that they had gone horseback riding a few times, but it was nothing serious. I knew she was the girl for me.

In the 1940s, most people double dated or met in groups at the movies or the skating rink downtown. Not all families had cars and those who did had only one. Almost everyone rode buses, even dating couples. With so few cars available, anyone who got to use the family automobile was expected to ask another couple to share in their good fortune. As a consequence, being together alone—just the two of us—was rare.

Velta lived on North Ninth and I lived across town when we started dating. When I realized she liked me, I made sure we were together every day on the bus to and from school. Even though my family lived close enough for me to walk to the high school, I got up each morning at 6:00 AM to catch the bus to the transfer station at Miller Drug Store. After meeting her, we rode the bus together to school. I just reversed my steps in the afternoon, sometimes accompanying her on a third bus to her house before heading home. We spent every weekend together after the first few weeks. I finally kissed her one evening in front of her house. I was hooked. She was the first girl I had kissed since I had been diagnosed with tuberculosis four years earlier.

For the rest of our senior year, we were a couple, always together. On the evenings when I couldn't see her, we talked for hours on the phone, being careful what we said. In those days, everyone had a telephone party line—a shared phone line among neighbors—and you could never tell who might be listening.

Most Saturdays, we went out to the 77 Ranch and rented horses to ride—a skill most girls in Wichita Falls lacked. On Friday or Saturday nights, we and the other couples in our group had a choice of the Majestic, Strand, Wichita, State, Texan, Gem, Ritz, Tower, and Monroe Street movie theaters to attend. Admission was twenty-five cents for adults and ten cents for kids under the age of twelve. If the movie had started, an usher in a cap and coat guided latecomers with a flashlight to a seat. Before or after the movie, we walked to a little cafe just a block over on Ohio Street for hamburgers and milk shakes. Hamburgers were three for a quarter and they were big. Milk shakes were fifteen cents. It didn't take a lot of money to date in the early 1940s—only a couple of dollars including bus fare.

Teenagers on dates talked to each other—a lot. There were no portable radios or televisions; and most of the time we were without a car. Velta and I talked about everything—our families, growing up, the war, our ambitions, and religion. The more I learned about her, the more I realized how much I wanted to spend the rest of my life with her. She was the only person I ever told about the loneliness of the sanatorium or living with a tuberculosis death sentence.

With the uncertainty of the war, most of my friends seemed to fall in and out of love on a weekly basis. It was different for me. I never loved anyone but Velta; she was my first, and my only love. We were married September 26, 1943, and moved to Dallas where I worked on the railroad. She told me she was pregnant the week before I left for training.

I don't remember much about the weekend leaves in Little Rock except for the personal things that should only be shared between man and wife. I was ecstatic to see her and hated to see her go home. We had one more weekend before training was over and it was just as good as our earlier visit and more difficult to see her go.

The last weeks of training seemed to fly by—filled with more drills and news about the European front. The Russians had begun a surge into Europe in chase of the Germans who had invaded their homeland. A second landing on the shores of France to liberate Paris by America and Great Britain was launched in August 1944. The general feeling among the trainees was that the tide had turned and the war with Germany would soon be over. The Pacific War continued to rage and we learned about the battle of Saipan, an island in the Central Pacific Ocean. With less than 1000 soldiers alive of the 30,000 that began the battle, the Japanese determined to fight to the death before surrendering. Even the Japanese civilians who lived on the island committed suicide rather than give up.

My concern intensified about where I might be sent. The Marines, part of the Navy, were primarily involved in the Pacific to begin with, rather than the Army. I think this was initially due to the smaller battles fought island to island. The Marines were trained for amphibious assaults while the Army fought large land battles. As things heated up in the Pacific, more Army units became involved. When I finished my sixteen weeks of training, I was given a week's leave, a new dress uniform, and a train ticket to Ft. Dix in New Jersey—a sure sign I was going to Germany. Soldiers destined for the Pacific shipped out of the West Coast.

I caught the first train to Dallas and then Wichita Falls in an attempt to surprise the family the next morning. Velta was living with Mother, Dad, and my sister Jean in their two-bedroom house in the middle of town. Many of their neighbors had sons in the service. As I walked from the bus stop to our house in my uniform, older and younger women came from their houses and yards to give me hugs and handshakes. Somebody must have called Mother because Velta came flying around the corner bare-footed in a nightgown with her untied robe streaming behind her. Unable to match her speed, Dad and Mother walked behind her. I dropped my duffle bag and swept her into my arms, just like in the movies. We were still embracing when Mother came up. I put Velta on the ground and hugged her, then shook Dad's hand. As Mother and Velta cried, their arms still around me, Dad reached out to pat me on the shoulder. "I'm glad you're home, Son," he said, stooping to grab my dropped bag.

That week was one of the happiest times of my life. I had never accomplished anything—taking an extra year to graduate and being arrested for drunkenness during high school in Childress. I knew I had not been the son Mom and Dad expected. But that week wiped away the past. For the first time, Dad treated me like a man—solicited my opinions and invited me to meet his friends at the downtown domino parlor. Mother hovered over me like I was sick—jumped to her feet to fix something to eat or bring me a cup of coffee every time I looked at her. My little sister Jean, who was just entering high school, introduced me to her giggling girl friends as if I were Clark Gable, King of the Silver Screen. Jean's attitude really surprised me since she had to spend the week with a friend so Velta and I could have the bedroom to ourselves.

Naturally slender, her pregnancy was just beginning to show. She complained that she was fat, but I thought she was more beautiful than ever. When she asked me if I wanted a girl or boy, I answered truthfully that I did not care. She was sure she was carrying a boy and had begun to think about names. I wasn't keen on the male names in my family—Jimmy, Virgil, Homer, Coke—but cared even less for the male names on her side—Albert, Odell, and Ralph. She was so sure she was carrying a boy that she never considered girl names. She told me she had started a list of boy names and would look up their meaning to ensure we picked the perfect name for our son. I trusted her judgment. When I left for Ft. Dix, the name was still uncertain.

The evening before I was to depart on the train to Ft. Dix, Mother called me into the kitchen for a private conversation. We sat down and she grabbed my hand. I remembered the other time when she and I had a serious talk. It was during my eighth grade year. She told me I had tuberculosis and would be sent to the sanatorium. I was worried that this might be more bad news.

"I just wanted to tell you that I've prayed to God about your going and to watch over you," she said. Mother was very religious and confident in her faith that God watched over her and her family. "I know you will come home to us unharmed. I think God has something in mind for you, especially since He cured you of tuberculosis."

I knew why she was talking to me alone. My dad, lacking Mother's faith, did not believe in miracles. He blamed the old Childress doctor for the misdiagnosis. I remembered their reaction after the Army physical when I told them I didn't have TB. I felt guilty telling them I was healthy. I was afraid they would blame me for the hell the family had experienced after the diagnosis.

"Son, you have just told your mother and me the best news we have heard in five years. Of course, we are not mad at you or blame you for what happened. If there is anyone to blame, it's that quack who said you had it in the first place. I'll make sure my friends in Childress know what an incompetent fake he really is." I knew Dad was really angry because he muttered a few curse words. I was happy he wasn't mad at me. "If I thought it would do any good, I'd go up there right now and whip his ass." His voice trailed off as he thought about it.

"Virgil, how can you say such things? God has performed a miracle for this family. He gave us our son back. This is the time you should fall on knees in gratitude, not have anger in your heart. I want both of you to go to church with me tonight to praise God for the blessing he has given this family."

Dad and I knew from the tone of her voice and the set of her jaw that arguing would be futile. I did not have a problem giving thanks to God, but I tended to agree with Dad that the experience was more likely due to a misdiagnosis than a miracle cure. I kept my opinion to myself. I did not know what to believe. On the one hand, I had never felt sick or had difficulties breathing, a common symptom with tuberculosis. The doctor in Childress who diagnosed me initially was old and his x-ray equipment was old. He easily could have made a mistake that cost me six months in the sanatorium and my family almost four years of separation and segregation from old friends. Dad clearly thought the doctor was to blame, but I was not sure.

If the Childress doctor was wrong, how could the doctors in the San Angelo sanatorium have missed it also? For six months, I saw doctors and nurses every day who worked closely with TB victims. If I was healthy and did not have the disease, it seems likely that someone would have raised objections about my quarantine. I spent twenty-four hours a day, seven days a week with other TB victims. Death was always present in the sanatorium; patients moved from the sanatorium to the hospital to their homes for their last days. It did not seem logical that I was checked several times a day, every day, without anyone questioning whether I had TB if that was not the case. I was confused.

I grew up in the Christian church. I went to church and Sunday school every week without fail for as long as I could remember. Mother's family included several preachers in previous generations, so faith in God was as much a part of me as loving my family. I believed that I was going to Heaven, but I did not think that miracles happened in modern times. Mother thought God had answered her prayers for my cure. Maybe he did, but that was hard for me to accept. If God acts in people's daily lives, why had I gotten sick in the first place? I was the only one in the town of Childress to be diagnosed with tuberculosis that year. Why me? Did God have a plan for me? Was I supposed to learn a lesson from having the dreaded disease that would prove useful or necessary in the future? Was it punishment for something I had done?

Answers eluded me. At the sanatorium, I had lain in bed for hours at a time thinking about my childhood and what I was likely to miss due to an early death. Over the next decade, I spent many more hours trying to decipher and understand the events of those years without coming to any conclusions. Mother believed that bad things happen because there is evil in the world—sometimes in the form of a man like Hitler, sometimes in the temptations that we face in our lives. She felt that being a Christian meant accepting whatever happened and making the best of it since it is all part of God's plan for us. I sometimes envied her faith. In the end, I had to settle for not knowing for sure what had happened: my heart told me that Mother was right and God had saved me while my head blamed an incompetent doctor with bad equipment.

I did not have a better answer when I boarded the train to Ft. Dix the next morning.

"An Unsung Hero: Sniper's Target" will be available in eBook, paperback, and audio versions by October 15, 2014.

CPSIA information can be obtained
at www.ICGtesting.com
Printed in the USA
BVHW041945290621
610751BV00014B/427